Annual Index

Series Editor: Cara Acred

Complete A-Z index listings for all
69 *Issues* titles currently in print

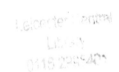

Independence Educational Publishers

First published by Independence Educational Publishers

The Studio, High Green

Great Shelford

Cambridge CB22 5EG

England

© Independence 2012

Copyright

Photocopy licence

British Library Cataloguing in Publication Data

Issues annual index 2012.

1. Issues--Indexes. 2. Social problems--Indexes.

I. Acred, Cara.

016.3'61-dc23

ISBN-13: 978 1 86168 6336

Printed in Great Britain

MWL Print Group Ltd

10:23 campaign against homeopathy **195**.31, 32
12 Step programmes **184**.30; **203**.25
40 Days for Life campaign **231**.34, 35

A

A&E departments and self-harm **199**.13-14
A-levels (Advanced Level)
    as predictor of degree performance **209**.12; **219**.32
abortion **231**.1-39
    aborted fetuses in stem cell trials **211**.33
    alternatives to **231**.8, 17-18
    anti-abortion campaigns **231**.34-5
    arguments against (pro-life) **231**.1, 16
    arguments for (pro-choice) **231**.1, 16
    counselling **231**.24-5, 26-9, 31, 36-7
    and disability **231**.20
    effects **231**.5, 6-7
        on men **231**.9
        on mental health **231**.14-15
    ethical issues **231**.16-29
    and the law **231**.1-2, 3, 32
    private clinics
        and advertising **231**.38
        and counseling **231**.24-5
        gender abortion **231**.30-31
        NHS funding **231**.24
    procedure **231**.6-7
    reasons for abortions **231**.13, 32
    religious positions on **231**.19
    risks **231**.6-7
    sex-selection abortion **231**.18, 30-31
    statistics **173**.3, 9; **182**.2, 29; **231**.10-12
    and teenage pregnancies **173**.3, 9; **182**.2, 12-13, 29
        making the decision **182**.6, 9
    time limit **231**.21-3
Abortion Act 1967 **231**.1
absenteeism
    sickness absence **183**.8, 9
    and work-life balance **183**.17
absolute poverty **235**.1, 2-3
abstinence education **173**.37
abuse
    effect on children **166**.35
    and children's mental health **201**.3
    class-based **219**.5-6
    see also domestic abuse; emotional abuse; neglect;
    physical abuse; sexual abuse
abusers
    domestic, help for **224**.39
    see also paedophiles
academic learning style in schools **209**.2
academic testing, racial differences **172**.14, 16
Academies Programme **209**.25, 26
    and social mobility **219**.28
Acceptable Daily Intake (ADI), food additives **205**.15
access rights, disabled people
    to goods and services **197**.21, 25
    public transport **197**.23
    to work **197**.21, 24
access to children *see* contact
Access to Work **197**.21
accidents
    alcohol-related **176**.15
    falls, older people **159**.4, 6
    road accidents **200**.12
    young people **176**.4
achievement *see* educational achievement
acidification of oceans **193**.30
acne **176**.20
active euthanasia **217**.5
activity, physical
Acts of Parliament **175**.18
    see also legislation
adaptive dysfunction **197**.6
addictions
    cannabis **186**.1, 10-11, 29
    Facebook **230**.15
    gambling **203**.6, 20
    see also problem gambling

Vol. numbers appear first (in bold) followed by page numbers; a change in volume is preceded by a semi-colon.

Vol. 159	An Ageing Population	**Vol. 189**	The Homeless Population	**Vol. 212**	International Terrorism
Vol. 161	Waste Issues	**Vol. 190**	Coping with Depression	**Vol. 213**	The Armed Forces
Vol. 162	Staying Fit	**Vol. 191**	The Changing Family	**Vol. 214**	Vegetarian Diets
Vol. 164	The AIDS Crisis	**Vol. 192**	Bereavement and Grief	**Vol. 215**	Religion in Society
Vol. 166	Marriage and Cohabitation	**Vol. 193**	Endangered Species	**Vol. 216**	Tackling Climate Change
Vol. 168	Privacy and Surveillance	**Vol. 194**	Responsible Drinking	**Vol. 217**	Euthanasia and Assisted Suicide
Vol. 172	Racial and Ethnic Discrimination	**Vol. 195**	Alternative Medicine	**Vol. 218**	A Sustainable Future
Vol. 173	Sexual Health	**Vol. 196**	Censorship Issues	**Vol. 219**	Class and Social Mobility
Vol. 174	Selling Sex	**Vol. 197**	Living with Disability	**Vol. 220**	Population Growth and Migration
Vol. 175	Citizenship and Participation	**Vol. 198**	Sport and Society	**Vol. 221**	Equality and Gender Roles
Vol. 176	Health Issues for Young People	**Vol. 199**	Self-Harming and Suicide	**Vol. 222**	Tourism and Travel
Vol. 177	Crime in the UK	**Vol. 200**	Sustainable Transport	**Vol. 223**	Crime. Punishment and Justice
Vol. 178	Reproductive Ethics	**Vol. 201**	Mental Wellbeing	**Vol. 224**	Domestic and Relationship Abuse
Vol. 179	Tackling Child Abuse	**Vol. 202**	Child Exploitation	**Vol. 225**	LGBT Equality
Vol. 180	Money and Finances	**Vol. 203**	The Gambling Problem	**Vol. 226**	Globalisation and Trade
Vol. 181	The Housing Issue	**Vol. 204**	The Energy Crisis	**Vol. 227**	Ethics in Business
Vol. 182	Teenage Conceptions	**Vol. 205**	Nutrition and Diet	**Vol. 228**	Illegal Drug Use
Vol. 183	Work and Employment	**Vol. 206**	Coping with Stress	**Vol. 229**	Protecting Human Rights
Vol. 184	Understanding Eating Disorders	**Vol. 207**	Consumerism and Ethics	**Vol. 230**	Evolution of the Internet
Vol. 185	Student Matters	**Vol. 208**	Genetic Modification	**Vol. 231**	The Abortion Debate
Vol. 186	Cannabis Use	**Vol. 209**	Education and Society	**Vol. 232**	Bullying in our Society
Vol. 187	Health and the State	**Vol. 210**	The Media	**Vol. 233**	Exploring Animal Rights
Vol. 188	Tobacco and Health	**Vol. 211**	Biotechnology and Cloning	**Vol. 234**	Skin Deep - debating body image
				Vol. 235	The Poverty Crisis

Internet **230**.14, 16-18
nicotine **188**.10, 16
children **176**.13
shopping **207**.6
Additional Member System **175**.25
additives *see* food additives
additional paternity leave **221**.4-5
ADHD (attention deficit and hyperactivity disorder) **176**.30
adoption **178**.14-16; **182**.6, 8-9; **191**.18-25
adoption leave **183**.18
adoption process **191**.18-19
as alternative to abortion **231**.8, 17-18
same-sex couples **178**.9-10; **191**.22-5; **225**.34
adult children
living with parents **180**.23; **181**.4-5; **191**.26
supported by parents **191**.27-8
adult learners **209**.39
adult stem cells **211**.28, 29
adulterous consumption **161**.8-9
adultery **166**.13-14
advance decisions (medical treatment) **217**.13, 35-6
advance statements **217**.35
advertising
abortion clinics **231**.38
and age **196**.20
airbrushing and unrealistic body images **184**.23; **234**.24-6, 27-8
alcohol **194**.39
and children **207**.35-6, 37, 39; **234**.23
children's awareness of gambling advertising **203**.13
junk food **205**.38
media advertising spending **210**.15
online **230**.5
regulation and body confidence issues **234**.21
tobacco **188**.23
using disabled model **197**.10
228.25-6, 27
affordable housing **181**.36
in rural areas **181**.3
shortage of **181**.6, 29
Afghanistan conflict after death of Osama bin Laden

212.24-5
Africa
AIDS programmes **164**.7
child soldiers **202**.33, 37-9
criminalization of homosexuality **225**.39
gender inequality **221**.1
HIV/AIDS infection rates **164**.4
poverty rates **235**.23, 24
press freedom **196**.2
African communities in UK
HIV prevention campaigns **164**.24-5
late HIV diagnosis **164**.17
age
and advertising **196**.20
and alcohol consumption **176**.3, 14; **194**.1-2, 30
and alcohol-related deaths **194**.13
and attachment to British identity **175**.9
and career fulfillment **183**.6
and child labour **202**.3, 16
and child soldiers **202**.33-4
and childhood aggression **224**.23
of criminal responsibility **223**.30, 31-2
and depression **190**.5, 22-3
at divorce **191**.8
in domestic violence definition **224**.35-6
and drinking behaviour, young people **194**.2
and employment, young people **180**.20
and fertility **178**.4
of first drink **194**.3
of first sexual intercourse **182**.1
of foetal viability **231**.21, 22
and IVF **178**.1, 19-20
at marriage **166**.4, 6; **191**.1
and risk of divorce **166**.28
retirement age **183**.14-15
of smokers **188**.1
age started smoking **188**.3
voting age lowering **175**.36-7, 39
age of consent **202**.16; **173**.1, 8, 11; **176**.21-2
age discrimination **159**.4, 8-13
in home care **229**.33

Vol. numbers appear first (in bold) followed by page numbers; a change in volume is preceded by a semi-**colon.**

Vol. 159   An Ageing Population
Vol. 161   Waste Issues
Vol. 162   Staying Fit
Vol. 164   The AIDS Crisis
Vol. 166   Marriage and Cohabitation
Vol. 168   Privacy and Surveillance
Vol. 172   Racial and Ethnic Discrimination
Vol. 173   Sexual Health
Vol. 174   Selling Sex
Vol. 175   Citizenship and Participation
Vol. 176   Health Issues for Young People
Vol. 177   Crime in the UK
Vol. 178   Reproductive Ethics
Vol. 179   Tackling Child Abuse
Vol. 180   Money and Finances
Vol. 181   The Housing Issue
Vol. 182   Teenage Conceptions
Vol. 183   Work and Employment
Vol. 184   Understanding Eating Disorders
Vol. 185   Student Matters
Vol. 186   Cannabis Use
Vol. 187   Health and the State
Vol. 188   Tobacco and Health
Vol. 189   The Homeless Population
Vol. 190   Coping with Depression
Vol. 191   The Changing Family
Vol. 192   Bereavement and Grief
Vol. 193   Endangered Species
Vol. 194   Responsible Drinking
Vol. 195   Alternative Medicine
Vol. 196   Censorship Issues
Vol. 197   Living with Disability
Vol. 198   Sport and Society
Vol. 199   Self-Harming and Suicide
Vol. 200   Sustainable Transport
Vol. 201   Mental Wellbeing
Vol. 202   Child Exploitation
Vol. 203   The Gambling Problem
Vol. 204   The Energy Crisis
Vol. 205   Nutrition and Diet
Vol. 206   Coping with Stress
Vol. 207   Consumerism and Ethics
Vol. 208   Genetic Modification
Vol. 209   Education and Society
Vol. 210   The Media
Vol. 211   Biotechnology and Cloning
Vol. 212   International Terrorism
Vol. 213   The Armed Forces
Vol. 214   Vegetarian Diets
Vol. 215   Religion in Society
Vol. 216   Tackling Climate Change
Vol. 217   Euthanasia and Assisted Suicide
Vol. 218   A Sustainable Future
Vol. 219   Class and Social Mobility
Vol. 220   Population Growth and Migration
Vol. 221   Equality and Gender Roles
Vol. 222   Tourism and Travel
Vol. 223   Crime. Punishment and Justice
Vol. 224   Domestic and Relationship Abuse
Vol. 225   LGBT Equality
Vol. 226   Globalisation and Trade
Vol. 227   Ethics in Business
Vol. 228   Illegal Drug Use
Vol. 229   Protecting Human Rights
Vol. 230   Evolution of the Internet
Vol. 231   The Abortion Debate
Vol. 232   Bullying in our Society
Vol. 233   Exploring Animal Rights
Vol. 234   Skin Deep - debating body image
Vol. 235   The Poverty Crisis

young people **159**.12
age limits for gambling, children's knowledge of **203**.13
age ratings
    lads' magazines **174**.28, 31
    video games **196**.17
age structure of population, global **220**.8
ageing
    ageing process **159**.1-2, 31-2
    attitude to **159**.14-15
    benefits of exercise **159**.33; **162**.12
    and health **159**.31-9
    effect of lifestyle **159**.33, 34
ageing population
    global **159**.5, 6; **220**.8
    UK **159**.3
ageism *see* age discrimination
agentist capitalism **226**.22, 23
aggressive behaviour in children **224**.22-3
agriculture
    and animal welfare **233**.2, 3
    and climate change **216**.11
    cotton farming **202**.13-14
    environmental impact **214**.16, 17, 22-3
    factory farming **233**.3, 7-8
    fairtrade *see* fair trade
    fur farming **233**.18, 19
    mega-farms **233**.3, 9-11
    subsidies, impact on developing countries **226**.33
    sustainable meat production **214**.14, 20-21, 23
    see also animal welfare; food production; genetically
    modified (GM) crops; organic farming
aid
    aid for trade **226**.34
    definitions **235**.32
    effectiveness **235**.31-2
    and gay rights **225**.14
    and slums **235**.38
AIDS (Acquired Immune Deficiency Syndrome) **164**.1, 2
    AIDS-related illnesses **164**.2
    anti-AIDS campaigns **164**.23-5
    'cures' **164**.37-8
    older people as carers **159**.5
    orphans **164**.6, 7
    treatments *see* anti-retroviral therapy (ART)
    see also HIV (Human Immunodeficiency Virus)
air pollution *see* emissions
air source heat pumps **204**.35
air travel
    air passenger duty tax **222**.14-15
    disabled people **197**.12
    emissions from **200**.14, 24
    environmental impact **200**.24-5
    and UK travel trends **161**.32
airbrushing and body image **234**.5, 18, 24-6, 27-8
aircraft carriers and defence budget cuts **213**.21
al-Qaida
    and Afghanistan conflict **212**.24-5
    after death of Osama bin Laden **212**.23
    terrorist attacks in Great Britain **212**.6
alcohol
    and accidents **176**.15

advertising **194**.39
    binge drinking *see* binge drinking
    calorie content **205**.5
    consumption
        children **194**.25-6
        myths **194**.16
        reducing **194**.5, 16, 23
        social drinkers **194**.17
        women **194**.7
        young people **194**.1-2
    and crime **194**.19-20, 21, 29
    deaths related to **194**.13
    and dementia **201**.10
    and domestic violence **224**.6
    drink spiking **194**.8-10
    drinking behaviour
        binge drinking **194**.22-3
        children **194**.25-6
        and knowledge of safe drinking guidelines **194**.34
        social drinking **194**.17
        young people **194**.2-3, 24
    and eating disorders **184**.16
    effects of **176**.4, 5, 15; **194**.6-7, 9, 22-3
        on appearance **194**.6
        on behaviour **194**.19-20
        effects on others **194**.15, 27-8
    health benefits of **194**.18
    health risks of **194**.6, 7, 15, 17, 18
        binge drinking **194**.22-3
        mental health effects **194**.6
        social drinking **194**.17
        young people **194**.19
    and hydration **205**.28
    and the law
        24-hour drinking **194**.20
        see also drink-driving
    and pregnancy **194**.14
    and sex **173**.15
    and smoking **188**.10
    and stress **206**.33
    and students **185**.9, 10
    underage drinking **176**.17-18; **194**.1-3, 25
        see also young people and alcohol
    units of **176**.15; **194**.4-5, 14
        recommended limits **194**.8, 14, 18
    see also binge drinking; young people and alcohol
alcohol abuse **194**.22-39
    and crime **194**.21, 29
    effects on family **194**.27-8
    help **194**.23
    and homeless people **189**.10-11, 13
    and mental illness **201**.17
        see also dual diagnosis
    risks **194**.22-3, 27-8
    signs of **194**.30
    statistics **194**.30
    see also underage drinking
alcohol-related brain impairment **201**.10
algae biofuels **204**.34
alien invasive species **193**.12
    UK **193**.38-9

allergies and food additives **205**.15
alternative medicine **195**.1-39
    buying habits **195**.8
    definition **195**.1
    herbal medicines **195**.9-13
    reasons for using **195**.5, 6-7
    safety **195**.2
    types **195**.3-5
    see also homeopathy
alternative tourism **222**.16
    definition **222**.24
    see also ecotourism; voluntourism
aluminium recycling **161**.22, 27
Alzheimer's disease **159**.4, 36-9
    and animal research **233**.36
Amazon forest destruction and cattle ranching **193**.14
Amazon town banning tourists **222**.32
ambulance trusts **187**.5-6
Americas, press freedom **196**.2
amino acids and GM food **208**.20
Amnesty International, response to UK counter-terrorism
review **212**.38-9
Amy Winehouse Foundation **228**.10-11
anabolic steroids **198**.29-30; **228**.26
anal sex and conception **182**.4
analgesics **198**.28-9
anger management **199**.6; **206**.3
Anglican Church and abortion **231**.19
animal cloning **211**.7-21
    Dolly the sheep **211**.7, 8
    ethical concerns **211**.10-11
    for food production **211**.6, 10-19
animal experimentation **233**.3, 28-39
    alternatives to **233**.28, 32
    and animal welfare societies **233**.1
    arguments against **233**.35-6
    arguments for **233**.37-8
    and genetically modified animals **211**.37-8
    myths and facts **233**.30-33
    reasons for **233**.28
    regulation of **233**.28, 33

    types of animals used **233**.29, 33
animal feed, GM content **208**.8, 24
animal fights **233**.6, 17, 27
animal rights
    whales and dolphins **233**.20-21
    see also animal welfare
animal welfare **233**.1-6
    circuses **233**.14-15
    and cloning **211**.10, 19
    and farming **233**.7-11
    and fur trade **233**.3-4, 18-19
    UK legislation on **233**.1-2, 5-6
    and vegetarianism **214**.5
Animal Welfare Act **233**.2, 5-6
    and film classification **196**.14
animals
    genetic modification *see* genetically modified animals
    homosexual behaviour **225**.15
anniversaries and grief **192**.5, 10, 20
annual percentage rate (APR) **180**.26
anorexia nervosa **184**.1, 3-4, 38-9
    causing death of model **234**.36
    link with brain development **184**.28
Antabuse **203**.27
Antarctic ice sheet and climate change **216**.12
anti-abortion campaigns **231**.34-5
antibiotic use in farming **233**.7
anti-bullying policies
    schools **232**.18
    and sexuality **232**.15
anti-bullying strategies **232**.3-4, 16, 19-21
    cyberbullying **232**.26-7, 28, 29, 39
    schools **232**.3, 10, 18
anti-depressant drugs **190**.10-11, 32-3; **206**.3
    and anxiety **206**.13
    and bipolar disorder **190**.10-11
    having little effect on mild depression **190**.36
    and seasonal affective disorder **190**.7
    and suicide **190**.24
    see also drug treatments for depression
anti-gay abuse, football **198**.26

Vol. numbers appear first (in bold) followed by page numbers; a change in volume is preceded by a semi-**colon**.

Vol. 159	An Ageing Population	**Vol. 189**	The Homeless Population	**Vol. 212**	International Terrorism
Vol. 161	Waste Issues	**Vol. 190**	Coping with Depression	**Vol. 213**	The Armed Forces
Vol. 162	Staying Fit	**Vol. 191**	The Changing Family	**Vol. 214**	Vegetarian Diets
Vol. 164	The AIDS Crisis	**Vol. 192**	Bereavement and Grief	**Vol. 215**	Religion in Society
Vol. 166	Marriage and Cohabitation	**Vol. 193**	Endangered Species	**Vol. 216**	Tackling Climate Change
Vol. 168	Privacy and Surveillance	**Vol. 194**	Responsible Drinking	**Vol. 217**	Euthanasia and Assisted Suicide
Vol. 172	Racial and Ethnic Discrimination	**Vol. 195**	Alternative Medicine	**Vol. 218**	A Sustainable Future
Vol. 173	Sexual Health	**Vol. 196**	Censorship Issues	**Vol. 219**	Class and Social Mobility
Vol. 174	Selling Sex	**Vol. 197**	Living with Disability	**Vol. 220**	Population Growth and Migration
Vol. 175	Citizenship and Participation	**Vol. 198**	Sport and Society	**Vol. 221**	Equality and Gender Roles
Vol. 176	Health Issues for Young People	**Vol. 199**	Self-Harming and Suicide	**Vol. 222**	Tourism and Travel
Vol. 177	Crime in the UK	**Vol. 200**	Sustainable Transport	**Vol. 223**	Crime. Punishment and Justice
Vol. 178	Reproductive Ethics	**Vol. 201**	Mental Wellbeing	**Vol. 224**	Domestic and Relationship Abuse
Vol. 179	Tackling Child Abuse	**Vol. 202**	Child Exploitation	**Vol. 225**	LGBT Equality
Vol. 180	Money and Finances	**Vol. 203**	The Gambling Problem	**Vol. 226**	Globalisation and Trade
Vol. 181	The Housing Issue	**Vol. 204**	The Energy Crisis	**Vol. 227**	Ethics in Business
Vol. 182	Teenage Conceptions	**Vol. 205**	Nutrition and Diet	**Vol. 228**	Illegal Drug Use
Vol. 183	Work and Employment	**Vol. 206**	Coping with Stress	**Vol. 229**	Protecting Human Rights
Vol. 184	Understanding Eating Disorders	**Vol. 207**	Consumerism and Ethics	**Vol. 230**	Evolution of the Internet
Vol. 185	Student Matters	**Vol. 208**	Genetic Modification	**Vol. 231**	The Abortion Debate
Vol. 186	Cannabis Use	**Vol. 209**	Education and Society	**Vol. 232**	Bullying in our Society
Vol. 187	Health and the State	**Vol. 210**	The Media	**Vol. 233**	Exploring Animal Rights
Vol. 188	Tobacco and Health	**Vol. 211**	Biotechnology and Cloning	**Vol. 234**	Skin Deep - debating body image
				Vol. 235	The Poverty Crisis

anti-Muslim attitudes **172**.24
    hate crime **215**.28-30
anti-obesity campaigns, potential harm **184**.33
anti-psychotic drugs **190**.10
anti-retroviral therapy (ART) **164**.2-3, 8-9, 29, 30-32
    during pregnancy **164**.29-30, 31
    worldwide access to **164**.39
anti-Semitism **172**.24-5; **215**.36
anti-social behaviour and alcohol **194**.19-20
Anti-terrorism Crime and Security Act 2001 **212**.19
anti-vivisection societies **233**.1
anxiety **206**.10-15
    causes **206**.11-12
    definition **206**.10, 14
    medication **206**.13
    and mortality **190**.20
    symptoms of **206**.10-11
appearance
    effects of alcohol **194**.6
    young smokers' concerns **188**.14
apprenticeships **183**.29, 38; **209**.38
    gender segregation **221**.28
approved mental health professionals **201**.38
aptitude tests for university admission **219**.32
Arab Spring and human rights violations **229**.9
Armed Forces **213**.1-39
    Armed Forces Covenant **213**.25-7, 28
    Army life **213**.1-2
    deaths **213**.9
    ex-service personnel *see* ex-service personnel
    injured personnel **213**.7, 8-9, 10-11
    and mental health **213**.3-6
    post traumatic stress disorder **213**.3-4, 5, 34
    restructuring **213**.17-19, 22-3
    and sexual orientation, USA **225**.38-9
    Strategic Defence and Security Review **213**.17-21
    Territorial Army **213**.30
    and women **213**.12-14
    and young people **213**.15-16
arranged marriages **166**.16
arrests
    British nationals overseas **222**.15
    at football matches **198**.13
arthritis, young people **197**.16–17
artificial wombs **178**.1-2
asbestos disposal **161**.23
Asda, plastic bags **161**.14
Asia
    child soldiers **202**.33
    criminalization of homosexuality **225**.39
    poverty rates **235**.23, 24, 25
Asia-Pacific region, press freedom **196**.2
Asian people in football **198**.24
assaults
    equal protection for children **179**.31-2
    on school staff **209**.16
assisted dying
    arguments for **217**.38-9
    legislation **217**.2
    see also assisted suicide; euthanasia
Assisted Dying for the Terminally Ill bill **217**.2

assisted reproductive technologies (ART) **178**.11-12
    ethical concerns **178**.11-12
    health problems for twins **178**.21-2
    see also in vitro fertilisation
assisted suicide **217**.5
    arguments against **217**.3-4
    arguments for **217**.3
    cases **217**.20, 21
    and disabled people **199**.39
    doctors' opposition to **217**.22
    legal guidelines **199**.37-8
    physician-assisted suicide **217**.22, 24-5
    prevalence in UK **217**.24-5
    public attitudes to **217**.23, 34
    see also assisted dying; euthanasia
asthma and exercise **198**.23
asylum seekers
    destitution **189**.14-15
    young,and mental health problems **201**.2
athletes
    drinking behaviour of stars, effect on young people
    198.14
    and drugs *see* drugs in sport
    punishment for missing drugs tests **198**.39
    talent identification **198**.8-10, 22
Attendance Allowance **197**.32-4
attention deficit and hyperactivity disorder (ADHD)
    176.30
audio media trends, international **210**.15
Australia
    compulsory voting **175**.29
    Internet censorship **196**.30
    regulation of prostitution **174**.13
    transgender rights **225**.24
Autoclave waste sorting system **161**.25
aversion therapy for homosexual behaviour **225**.16
aviation *see* air travel

B

babies, premature, viability **231**.21, 22
bacterial vaginosis (BV) **173**.17
bail, in Legal Aid, Sentencing and Punishment of Offenders
Bill **223**.25
balance of excellence, sport **198**.37
balanced diet *see* healthy eating
ballot papers **175**.24, 26
banana trade **226**.35
Bangkok climate change negotiations **216**.37
banks **180**.25-7
    bail-outs **227**.16
    banking crisis **180**.4
  borrowing from **180**.26-7
    informing of a death **192**.32
  opening an account **180**.25
    and personal information **168**.8
    student accounts **185**.2-3
    taxation **235**.13-15
    use of tax havens **227**.36

batteries
    potato-powered **204**.39
    recycling **161**.23, 28
battery farmed chickens **233**.3, 7
BBC
    Choosing to Die documentary **217**.20
    Editorial Guidelines **210**.27
    Ofcom regulation **196**.20
    radio and TV services **210**.3
BDD *see* body dysmorphic disorder
bears, reintroduction into Britain **193**.33-4
beavers, reintroduction into Britain **193**.34
bed and breakfast hotels, homeless families **189**.8
bees, declining numbers **193**.27-8
begging **189**.18-20
    giving to beggars **189**.35-6
behaviour
    effects of alcohol **194**.19-20, 23
    pupils, and teacher stress **209**.15
    signs of drug use **228**.15
    stress and behavioural changes **206**.19
benefits *see* state benefits
benzoic acid **205**.14
bereavement **192**.1-39
    children **192**.4, 5-6,9-19, 21; **201**.2
    complicated **192**.16-17
    feelings **192**.1-2, 3, 9-10, 11
    funerals **192**.30-31, 34-7
    memorial websites **192**.38-9
    parents **192**.20-23
    practical matters **192**.24-39
    support **192**.2, 4, 5-6
        children **192**.4, 5, 10, 17
        young people **192**.10, 12, 17
    young people **192**.9-19
betting **203**.4
    see also gambling
Big Brothel survey **174**.8-9
Big Issue **189**.37-9
bikes *see* cycling
bill payments and budgeting **180**.30-31

Bills (parliamentary) **175**.18
bin Laden, Osama, effect of death on al-Qaida **212**.23
binge drinking **194**.22-3
    effects **176**.15; **194**.22-3
    young people **176**.14-16
binge eating **184**.6-7, 35
bingo **203**.4
binoculars, recycling **161**.23
bioaccumulative chemicals **193**.16
Bio-Bug (methane-powered car) **204**.39
biochemical causes of depression **190**.2
biodegradability of litter **161**.16
biodegradable products, environmental impact **218**.37
biodiesel, from algae **204**.34
biodiversity
    conservation, marine environments **218**.22-3
    and ecotourism **222**.28
    and global economy **193**.10-12
    key scientific questions **193**.7
    loss **193**.13; **218**.14, 18
        England **193**.31-2
    and oil palm industry **193**.8-9
    public attitudes to **216**.11; **218**.17
    and tourism **222**.22-3, 28
    value of **193**.6
bioenergy *see* biomass energy
bio-fortification **208**.19
biofuels **204**.3, 26, 32, 39; **208**.22
    from algae **204**.34
biological causes of criminal behaviour **223**.11
biomass energy **204**.3, 6, 26
    Drax power plant **204**.5, 7
biomass heating **204**.3, 36
biomaterials **208**.21
biometrics
    biometric fingerprinting in schools **168**.30
    biometric travel documents **168**.13
    problems with **168**.18
biotech companies **208**.3-4, 24
biotechnology
    applications **211**.4

Vol. numbers appear first (in bold) followed by page numbers; a change in volume is preceded by a semi-**colon**.

Vol. 159 An Ageing Population
Vol. 161 Waste Issues
Vol. 162 Staying Fit
Vol. 164 The AIDS Crisis
Vol. 166 Marriage and Cohabitation
Vol. 168 Privacy and Surveillance
Vol. 172 Racial and Ethnic Discrimination
Vol. 173 Sexual Health
Vol. 174 Selling Sex
Vol. 175 Citizenship and Participation
Vol. 176 Health Issues for Young People
Vol. 177 Crime in the UK
Vol. 178 Reproductive Ethics
Vol. 179 Tackling Child Abuse
Vol. 180 Money and Finances
Vol. 181 The Housing Issue
Vol. 182 Teenage Conceptions
Vol. 183 Work and Employment
Vol. 184 Understanding Eating Disorders
Vol. 185 Student Matters
Vol. 186 Cannabis Use
Vol. 187 Health and the State
Vol. 188 Tobacco and Health

Vol. 189 The Homeless Population
Vol. 190 Coping with Depression
Vol. 191 The Changing Family
Vol. 192 Bereavement and Grief
Vol. 193 Endangered Species
Vol. 194 Responsible Drinking
Vol. 195 Alternative Medicine
Vol. 196 Censorship Issues
Vol. 197 Living with Disability
Vol. 198 Sport and Society
Vol. 199 Self-Harming and Suicide
Vol. 200 Sustainable Transport
Vol. 201 Mental Wellbeing
Vol. 202 Child Exploitation
Vol. 203 The Gambling Problem
Vol. 204 The Energy Crisis
Vol. 205 Nutrition and Diet
Vol. 206 Coping with Stress
Vol. 207 Consumerism and Ethics
Vol. 208 Genetic Modification
Vol. 209 Education and Society
Vol. 210 The Media
Vol. 211 Biotechnology and Cloning

Vol. 212 International Terrorism
Vol. 213 The Armed Forces
Vol. 214 Vegetarian Diets
Vol. 215 Religion in Society
Vol. 216 Tackling Climate Change
Vol. 217 Euthanasia and Assisted Suicide
Vol. 218 A Sustainable Future
Vol. 219 Class and Social Mobility
Vol. 220 Population Growth and Migration
Vol. 221 Equality and Gender Roles
Vol. 222 Tourism and Travel
Vol. 223 Crime. Punishment and Justice
Vol. 224 Domestic and Relationship Abuse
Vol. 225 LGBT Equality
Vol. 226 Globalisation and Trade
Vol. 227 Ethics in Business
Vol. 228 Illegal Drug Use
Vol. 229 Protecting Human Rights
Vol. 230 Evolution of the Internet
Vol. 231 The Abortion Debate
Vol. 232 Bullying in our Society
Vol. 233 Exploring Animal Rights
Vol. 234 Skin Deep - debating body image
Vol. 235 The Poverty Crisis

definition **211**.1, 4
history **211**.2-3
see also cloning; genetic modification
bipolar affective disorder (manic depression) **185**.8;
190.2, 8-11, 22; **201**.14-15, 24-5
causes **190**.9
diagnosis **190**.8
experiences of sufferers **201**.14-15
genetic factors **190**.11, 12-13
prevalence **190**.23
symptoms **190**.8-9
treatments **190**.10-11
types **190**.9-10
bird flu resistance, GM chickens **208**.14
birth control *see* contraception
birth rates
and abortion rate, UK **231**.11
global **220**.2, 4, 9, 13, 15
and marital status **191**.1
see also teenage pregnancies
bisexuality *see* LGBT people
Bishops in the House of Lords **175**.19; **215**.6
Black History Month **172**.22
black people
black identity **172**.31-2
women and poverty **221**.34
young people and mental health problems **201**.2
see also employment and racism; ethnic minorities; racism
blindness, disability classification **197**.1
blogging **210**.16
blood, effects of smoking **188**.7
blood donation
from gay and bisexual men **225**.36-7
and HIV **164**.1
blood doping **198**.29
blood pressure, effect of salt intake **205**.25
blood products and HIV **164**.1, 19-20, 25
blood tests
drug testing in sport **198**.27
for HIV diagnosis **164**.2, 20-21
BMA
and abortion counselling **231**.28, 29
vote against homeopathy funding **195**.16
BNP, inclusion in political debates **196**.7, 8
boardroom positions
gender quotas **221**.16, 21
women **221**.14, 15, 16, 17-18, 20, 21-2, 37
bodily privacy **168**.2
body confidence promotion
Girlguiding UK **234**.34
government campaign **234**.20-21, 37, 39
parent pack **234**.39
in schools **234**.11, 21, 29-30
body dysmorphic disorder/dysmorphophobia **184**.7
body image **184**.17-24; **234**.1-39
Barbie ideal **234**.31
and exercise **176**.7
and fashion industry **184**.24; **234**.5-6, 11
girls **184**.17-18, 27
improving **234**.1-3
and lads' magazines **174**.29

and the media **234**.5, 7, 8, 10, 11, 18
men **184**.20l **234**.13, 16-17
negative **234**.1
positive *see* body confidence promotion
public concerns over **184**.19-20
and young people **234**.7, 26
body mass index (BMI) **162**.1, 4, 23
and children **162**.1
criticism of **162**.5
and meat-eating **214**.35
body talk
men **234**.16-17
women **234**.8
body weight
effects of eating breakfast **205**.9
and fertility **178**.5
see also obesity; weight management
Bolivia
child labour **202**.9-10
education programme **229**.28
bone marrow transplants, saviour siblings **178**.28-9
bones, effect of cannabis use **186**.6, 29
bonuses
and inequality **227**.15
justification of **227**.19
books, self-help, mental health **190**.38
borrowing
from banks **180**.26-7
see also debt
botnets **196**.34
bottled waters, labelling rules **205**.11
bottom billion **235**.28-9
boxing, women **198**.19
boycotts, effect on child labour **202**.13
boys and young men
attitudes to sex **173**.12-13
and education
attitude to school **209**.11
single-sex schools **221**.30
and sex object culture **174**.27
toy preferences **221**.7-8
and parenthood **182**.17
brain
brain development and anorexia risk **184**.28
effects of cannabis on **186**.28-9
and placebo effect **195**.28-9
and sexual orientation **225**.15-16
brain damage and gambling **203**.7
brain drain **220**.32-3
brands
national versus store brands **207**.11
ownership of ethical brands **207**.31
Brazil
cattle ranching and deforestation **193**.14
censorship of sexual content on the Internet **196**.37
compulsory voting **175**.29
economic development **226**.20-21
bread, labelling rules **205**.11-12
breakfast
children going without **205**.8
consumer habits **205**.17

importance of **205**.9
breakfast clubs **205**.9
Breaking the Cycle Green Paper **223**.23
bribery and corruption in business **227**.31
Britain *see* UK
'Britain Day' proposal **175**.4-6
British Board of Film Classification (BBFC) **196**.13-16
    and legislation **196**.14
British Crime Survey **223**.3-5
British Heart Foundation and animal research **233**.36
British Homeopathic Association **195**.22
British identity **175**.3, 9, 10-11
    and social cohesion **175**.10
    young people **175**.12
British Medical Association, vote against homeopathy
funding **195**.16
British National Party, inclusion in political debates **196**.7, 8
British tourists
    arrested or hospitalised overseas **222**.15
    holidaying at home **222**.5
Britishness *see* British identity
broadband services **230**.6-8
    super-fast broadband **210**.15
broadcasters
    freedom of expression **196**.24
    regulation **196**.18-20; **210**.27
    see also radio; television
brothels **174**.6
    Big Brothel survey **174**.8-9
brownfield sites **181**.36
Bt plants **208**.3, 21
Buddhism **215**.1
    and abortion **231**.19
    funerals **192**.36
    meditation as treatment for depression **190**.35-6
    and vegetarianism **214**.6
Budget, the **175**.18; **180**.24
budgeting **180**.30-31
    for home buying **181**.24
    students **185**.3, 11

building industry *see* construction industry
building societies **180**.25-7
building waste recycling **161**.23
building your own home **181**.30-31
bulimia nervosa **184**.1, 4-5
bullfighting **233**.17
bullies
    characteristics of **232**.2
    consequences for **232**.22
bullying **232**.1-39
    children with gender-variant behaviour **225**.24
    cyber-bullying *see* cyberbullying
    dealing with bullying **232**.3, 17, 18, 19-21
        cyberbullying **232**.3, 26, 29, 39
        in the workplace **232**.23, 24
    and eating disorders **184**.8
    effects **232**.3, 8, 21, 22
        of cyberbullying **232**.25, 26
        on mental health **201**.2
    forms of bullying behaviour **232**.1, 21-2
    homophobic **225**.8, 9, 29; **232**.12-13, 15
    laws concerning **225**.7
        cyberbullying **232**.34-5, 37
    LGBT pupils **225**.8
    by mobile phone **232**.17, 25, 27, 29
    prevalence of **232**.30, 31
    punishment for **232**.22
    racist **172**.8; **232**.10, 11, 17
    reasons for **232**.2, 14, 25-6
    reporting **232**.20
        cyberbullying **232**.29, 36, 39
        workplace **232**.24
    sexual **221**.11
    signs of **232**.2-3
    and social media **227**.38; **232**.25, 26-7, 28
    statistics **232**.4
    and suicide **232**.9
    victims **232**.2, 8
    at work *see* workplace bullying
    see also bullies; school bullying; workplace
        bullying

Vol. numbers appear first (in bold) followed by page numbers; a change in volume is preceded by a semi-**colon.**

Vol. 159 An Ageing Population	**Vol. 189** The Homeless Population	**Vol. 212** International Terrorism
Vol. 161 Waste Issues	**Vol. 190** Coping with Depression	**Vol. 213** The Armed Forces
Vol. 162 Staying Fit	**Vol. 191** The Changing Family	**Vol. 214** Vegetarian Diets
Vol. 164 The AIDS Crisis	**Vol. 192** Bereavement and Grief	**Vol. 215** Religion in Society
Vol. 166 Marriage and Cohabitation	**Vol. 193** Endangered Species	**Vol. 216** Tackling Climate Change
Vol. 168 Privacy and Surveillance	**Vol. 194** Responsible Drinking	**Vol. 217** Euthanasia and Assisted Suicide
Vol. 172 Racial and Ethnic Discrimination	**Vol. 195** Alternative Medicine	**Vol. 218** A Sustainable Future
Vol. 173 Sexual Health	**Vol. 196** Censorship Issues	**Vol. 219** Class and Social Mobility
Vol. 174 Selling Sex	**Vol. 197** Living with Disability	**Vol. 220** Population Growth and Migration
Vol. 175 Citizenship and Participation	**Vol. 198** Sport and Society	**Vol. 221** Equality and Gender Roles
Vol. 176 Health Issues for Young People	**Vol. 199** Self-Harming and Suicide	**Vol. 222** Tourism and Travel
Vol. 177 Crime in the UK	**Vol. 200** Sustainable Transport	**Vol. 223** Crime. Punishment and Justice
Vol. 178 Reproductive Ethics	**Vol. 201** Mental Wellbeing	**Vol. 224** Domestic and Relationship Abuse
Vol. 179 Tackling Child Abuse	**Vol. 202** Child Exploitation	**Vol. 225** LGBT Equality
Vol. 180 Money and Finances	**Vol. 203** The Gambling Problem	**Vol. 226** Globalisation and Trade
Vol. 181 The Housing Issue	**Vol. 204** The Energy Crisis	**Vol. 227** Ethics in Business
Vol. 182 Teenage Conceptions	**Vol. 205** Nutrition and Diet	**Vol. 228** Illegal Drug Use
Vol. 183 Work and Employment	**Vol. 206** Coping with Stress	**Vol. 229** Protecting Human Rights
Vol. 184 Understanding Eating Disorders	**Vol. 207** Consumerism and Ethics	**Vol. 230** Evolution of the Internet
Vol. 185 Student Matters	**Vol. 208** Genetic Modification	**Vol. 231** The Abortion Debate
Vol. 186 Cannabis Use	**Vol. 209** Education and Society	**Vol. 232** Bullying in our Society
Vol. 187 Health and the State	**Vol. 210** The Media	**Vol. 233** Exploring Animal Rights
Vol. 188 Tobacco and Health	**Vol. 211** Biotechnology and Cloning	**Vol. 234** Skin Deep - debating body image
		Vol. 235 The Poverty Crisis

burial abroad **192**.31

burqa wearing
  arguments for and against **215**.37-8
  prohibition in European countries **215**.34-6
  public opinions **215**.39

bursaries, students **185**.2

buses
  bus lane on M4 **200**.36
  and disabled people **197**.11-12
  electric **200**.28-9
  guided busways **200**.30, 32
  straddling bus **200**.29
  usage **200**.3

bushmeat trade **193**.23

business ownership aspirations **183**.7; **227**.6

businesses **227**.1-39
  corporate responsibility **227**.9-30
  and economic growth **227**.14
  and higher education **185**.34-6
  new working practices **227**.1-3
  public attitudes to **227**.13-14
  start-ups **227**.5
  statistics **227**.4-5, 6
  and tax **227**.32-6

butterflies, declining numbers, Britain **193**.36

buying a home
  costs **181**.24
  disability rights **197**.21-2
  young people **181**.26
  see also home ownership

by-elections **175**.25

C

C.difficile **187**.28, 29

Cabinet, The **175**.20

CAES (Compressed Air Energy Storage) **204**.37-8

CAFCASS (Children and Family Court Advisory and Support Service) **166**.26, 36

calcium
  dietary sources **176**.8
  teenagers' requirements **176**.8
  and vegetarian diets **214**.29, 30, 33

calorie intake **162**.8
  teenagers **176**.8

Calthorpe Clinic, abortions **231**.30-31

Cambodia, child labour **202**.9

Cameron, David
  entrepreneurship campaign **227**.7
  on immigration policy **220**.30-31

Campaign Against Living Miserably (CALM) **199**.28

camping holidays, luxury **222**.20

Canada
  as gap year destination **222**.19
  seal hunting **233**.22, 23

candidates for parliamentary elections **175**.22-3, 26

cancer
  and alcohol consumption **194**.6
  and cannabis use **186**.16, 15; **228**.9

and complementary therapies **195**.6-7
  as disability **197**.1
  and passive smoking **188**.10-11
  and red meat consumption **214**.35
  and salt intake **205**.26
  skin **176**.10-11
  and smoking **188**.8-11
  and vegetarian diets **214**.38-9
  see also cervical cancer; lung cancer

Cancer Research UK, funding animal research **233**.35, 38

Cancun Agreement **226**.4

Cancun climate change conference **216**.37, 39

cannabinoids
  THC **186**.7, 9, 13, 22

cannabis **186**.1-39
  appearance **186**.2
  cannabis oil **186**.2, 7, 22
  cannabis resin (hashish) **186**.2, 7, 9
  chemical content **186**.7, 9
  classification **186**.4-5, 32
    see also reclassification
  compulsive use **186**.11
  cost **186**.2
  cultivation
    method, effect on potency **186**.22
    sentencing guidelines **228**.30-31
  effects of **186**.1, 3,37-8, 9-10, 28-9; **228**.14
    on bones **186**.6, 29
    on the brain **186**.28-9
    cancer healing claims **186**.16; **228**.9
    on education and learning **186**.9-10
    on family life **186**.23-5
    on lungs **186**.15, 28
    medicinal **186**.16-17
    skunk **186**.13
  forms of **186**.2, 7, 9
  giving up **186**.11
  and hard drug use **186**.29
  herbal cannabis (marijuana/grass) **186**.2, 9
  history **186**.3-4, 7, 16-17, 25
  and the law **186**.1-2, 5, 8, 9, 30-39
  legalisation debate **186**.4, 38-9
  medicinal use of **186**.16-17
  and mental health **186**.10-13, 16, 28-9, 30, 31, 32; **228**.8
  names for **186**.1
  penalties
    for possession **186**.1-2, 5, 9, 30
    sentencing guidelines **228**.28-9, 30-31
    for supply **186**.2, 30
  potency of **186**.2, 6, 21, 22
    skunk **186**.13
  production *see* cannabis cultivation
  psychosis **186**.10, 12, 31, 32
  purity **186**.2-3
  reclassification **186**.4-5, 32-3; 23
    public opinion **186**.31
  and schizophrenia **228**.8
  signs of use **228**.14
  THC (delta-9 tetrahydrocannabinol) **186**.7, 9, 13, 22
  use
    giving up **186**.11

worldwide **186**.18-19
canned hunting **193**.17
cans, recycling **161**.27
canvassers (elections) **175**.26
capitalism, defence of **227**.17, 18-19
car batteries, recycling **161**.28
car clubs **200**.11
car-free days **200**.19-20
carbon capture and storage **204**.27
carbon dioxide
    and GM crops **208**.20, 22
    rising levels, effects on oceans **193**.30
carbon dioxide emissions
    EU targets **204**.30
    and population growth **220**.14
    UK targets **204**.28-9
    see also greenhouse gas
carbon footprint, GM food **208**.29
carbon monoxide in tobacco smoke **188**.4, 7
carbon offsetting **216**.35-6
    and inequality **218**.3-4
    and rainforest protection **218**.20-21
cardboard recycling **161**.24, 26-7
cardiopulmonary resuscitation (CPR) **217**.13-14
cardiovascular disease
    caused by stress **206**.4
    and eating red meat **214**.35
    see also heart disease
care funding, personalization **197**.13
care homes **159**.27-8; **179**.10-11
care leavers
    and homelessness **189**.6
    housing rights **189**.25
care services for older people **159**.4
    concerns about **159**.28
    funding **159**.29
    and human rights **229**.33-4
    rising costs **159**.26
care trusts **187**.6
cared-for children and mental health problems **201**.3-4
career advice

failing young people **183**.39
career aspirations, and gender **221**.21, 28-9
career breaks **183**.18, 20
career fulfillment age **183**.6
carers
    experiencing grief **192**.6
    older people as carers **159**.4, 5
carrier bags *see* plastic bags
cars
    batteries, recycling **161**.28
    car clubs **200**.11
    congestion *see* congestion, traffic
    drink-driving *see* drink-driving
    electric **200**.26, 27; **204**.7
    emissions reduction **200**.15
    impact on health **200**.1, 23
    methane-powered **204**.39
    recycling **161**.23
    reducing use of **200**.7-8, 19-20, 25, 26
    sharing **200**.25
    usage trends **161**.31
    see also driving; road accidents
cartons, recycling **161**.23
cash cards **180**.13, 25
cash machine withdrawals **180**.16, 17
cash payments **180**.13
    statistics **180**.16-17
cashless society **180**.15-16
casinos
    being sued for gambler's losses **203**.38
    casino games **203**.4
cassava, genetically modified **208**.36
cassiterite **226**.3
casual sex, international comparisons **173**.6
Catholic Church
    and abortion **231**.19, 39
    and embryo research **178**.35
    and IVF **178**.17
    see also Christianity
cattle
    cloning **211**.12, 13-17

---

ranching and deforestation **193**.14
see also livestock farming
CBT *see* Cognitive Behavioural Therapy
CBT-E (enhanced cognitive behavioural therapy) and
eating disorders **184**.37-8
CCTV (Closed Circuit Television) **168**.6, 7, 8-9, 22-5
    and crime prevention **168**.23-4
    in schools **168**.25
    and sound recording **168**.24
    statistics **168**.22
celebrities
    and body image **234**.6-7
    and cyberbullying **232**.38
    libel actions **210**.38
cell ageing **159**.1
censorship
    films **196**.13, 14
    and the Internet **196**.27-39
    sexual content on the Internet **196**.36-8
census
    questions on national identity **175**.10-11
    religious belief data **215**.5
Central and Eastern Europe, press freedom **196**.2
Centre for Appearnce Research (CAR) **234**.4, 15
Centre for Separated Families **166**.31
cerebral palsy **197**.3-4
ceremonies, British **175**.2
certificates of identity **168**.13
cervical cancer
    screening **173**.39
    vaccination **173**.38-9
cetaceans' rights **233**.20-21
Chadwick, Edwin **219**.11
Chance to Shine cricket scheme **198**.3-4; **232**.7
character capabilities of children, factors affecting
191.6-7
character skills and children's attainment **219**.34-5
charities
    animal welfare **233**.1
    business support for **227**.20-21
    caring for wounded troops **213**.7
    fraud **207**.21, 22
    medical, funding animal research **233**.35-8
    poverty aid **235**.32
Charter Schools, USA **209**.20
chatrooms and bullying **232**.25, 36
chavs, prejudice against **219**.5
cheating in sport, childrens views on **198**.38
cheese production using GM organisms **208**.8
chelation therapy **195**.5
chemicals
    disposal **161**.23
    impact on wildlife **193**.16-17
    pollution from pharmaceutical waste **218**.38-9
    in tobacco smoke **188**.4, 9-10, 15
cheques **180**.13, 25
chewing tobacco **188**.11
chickens *see* hens
child abuse **179**.1-12
    emotional **179**.1; 5
    getting help **179**.5-6, 7

    help for professionals **179**.11-12
    images on the Internet **196**.39
    and mental health problems **201**.3
    neglect **179**.3, 5
        reporting **179**.7
        taking children into care **179**.10-11
    online **179**.15-16, 17
    physical **179**.1-2, 5
        see also corporal punishment; smacking
    prevalence **179**.4, 8-9, 13, 15, 17
    signs and symptoms **179**.5-6
    see also corporal punishment; paedophiles; sexual abuse;
smacking
child exploitation **202**.1-39
    definition **202**.1
    reasons for **202**.2
    see also child labour; sexual exploitation of children
Child Exploitation and Online Protection (CEOP) Centre
179.15-16
child labour **202**.1-15; **229**.15-16
    and age of child **202**.3, 16
    consumer influence **202**.13-14
    definitions **202**.3
    domestic labour **202**.12
    and education **202**.4-5; **221**.39
    elimination **202**.2, 4-5, 7-8, 15
    hazards **202**.4, 12
    numbers of child labourers **202**.3-4, 6-7
    reasons for **202**.5, 12
    tobacco pickers **188**.39
Child Labour Index **202**.11
child marriage **202**.19
child pornography **202**.17-18
    online **179**.17
child poverty **235**.5, 18-22
    and education **235**.21-2
    effects **235**.19
    quiz **235**.20
    statistics **235**.18-19
Child Poverty Act **235**.19
child prostitution **174**.11-12; **202**.17, 24-6
child safety orders **223**.32
child sex tourism **202**.18-19
child soldiers **202**.32-9
    girls **202**.32, 35-6
    numbers **202**.32-3
    punishment **202**.34
    rehabilitation **202**.36, 37-9
child trafficking **202**.1, 27-31
childbirth
    and exercise **162**.32
    see also post-natal depression
childcare
    and children's development **191**.16-17
    and fathers **221**.4-5
    financial help for young parents **182**.6
    gender gap **221**.6
    and grandparents **191**.15, 16-17
    and welfare reform bill **235**.9
childhood, children's rights to **229**.25
childhood obesity **162**.6, 13-14, 25-9; **176**.2, 3; **205**.19

effects of exercise **162**.28, 29
as neglect **162**.27
childhood problems
and suicide risk **199**.34
ChildLine
number of calls **181**.13
peer support project (CHIPS) **199**.33
and sex worries **173**.7
and sexual abuse **179**.13-15
and suicide **176**.35, 36-7; **199**.22, 31, 32, 33
ChildLine in Partnership with Schools (CHIPS) **199**.33
children
abuse *see* child abuse
and advertising **207**.35-6, 37, 39
aggressive behaviour **224**.22-3
alcohol consumption **176**.3, 14; **194**.1-3, 25-6
influence of household drinking habits **194**.25
of alcoholic parents **194**.27-8
anxiety and phobias **206**.13
attitudes to parents drinking **194**.28
bereavement **192**.4, 5-6, 13-19, 21
facts and figures **192**.12
support **192**.4, 5-6, 10, 17
character skills, importance of **219**.34-5
of cohabiting couples **166**.14-15
and the commercial world **207**.37-9
contact with parents after divorce **166**.37-8; **191**.11
cricket scheme, improving social well-being **198**.3-4
and crime **223**.30-32
sentences for riot crime **223**.29
death, children's understanding of **192**.4, 13, 15, 19
definition, in international conventions **202**.3, 16
development, effect of childcare **191**.16-17
development of character capabilities **191**.6-7
disabled *see* disabled children
discipline *see* discipline
and divorce **166**.4-5, 29-31, 34-8; **191**.1, 9
and domestic abuse **224**.24-6, 37
earning money **180**.20
exercise, lack of **162**.13, 15, 25
family background, effect on outcomes **219**.22, 23, 25-6,
27-8, 29-30, 34
fluid intake **205**.28
and food additives **205**.14-15
and food advertising **205**.38
and fuel poverty **235**.15-16
and gambling **203**.12-14
problem gambling **203**.20
gender-variant behaviour **225**.23-4
and grief **192**.4, 5-6, 19
health **176**.2-3
government strategy **162**.17
and healthy eating
breakfast **205**.8, 9
misleading marketing of children's foods **205**.39
packed lunches **205**.7, 10
healthy weight **162**.25
and HIV/AIDS **164**.6-8
preventing HIV transmission from mother **164**.25, 27,
29-30, 31
and homelessness **189**.29-32
housing problems **181**.13, 14
and the Internet **230**.4-5, 25, 33-4
LGBT children and schools **225**.5-8
life on the streets **189**.27-8
local authority responsibilities **224**.37
in lone parent families **191**.12
and the mediation process **166**.39
and mental health problems **201**.2-4
missing breakfast **205**.8, 9
obesity *see* childhood obesity
packed lunches **205**.7, 10
and passive smoking **188**.5, 11
and parental relationships **166**.32; **191**.1
and parental separation **166**.4-5, 29, 30, 31, 32; **191**.1, 8,
9; **201**.3
and poverty *see* child poverty
and prison *see* youth custody
rights of domestic abuse victims **224**.38
and self-harm **199**.17
sex, worries about **173**.7
sexual abuse *see* sexual abuse

Vol. numbers appear first (in bold) followed by page numbers; a change in volume is preceded by a semi-**colon**.

Vol. 159	An Ageing Population	**Vol. 189**	The Homeless Population
Vol. 161	Waste Issues	**Vol. 190**	Coping with Depression
Vol. 162	Staying Fit	**Vol. 191**	The Changing Family
Vol. 164	The AIDS Crisis	**Vol. 192**	Bereavement and Grief
Vol. 166	Marriage and Cohabitation	**Vol. 193**	Endangered Species
Vol. 168	Privacy and Surveillance	**Vol. 194**	Responsible Drinking
Vol. 172	Racial and Ethnic Discrimination	**Vol. 195**	Alternative Medicine
Vol. 173	Sexual Health	**Vol. 196**	Censorship Issues
Vol. 174	Selling Sex	**Vol. 197**	Living with Disability
Vol. 175	Citizenship and Participation	**Vol. 198**	Sport and Society
Vol. 176	Health Issues for Young People	**Vol. 199**	Self-Harming and Suicide
Vol. 177	Crime in the UK	**Vol. 200**	Sustainable Transport
Vol. 178	Reproductive Ethics	**Vol. 201**	Mental Wellbeing
Vol. 179	Tackling Child Abuse	**Vol. 202**	Child Exploitation
Vol. 180	Money and Finances	**Vol. 203**	The Gambling Problem
Vol. 181	The Housing Issue	**Vol. 204**	The Energy Crisis
Vol. 182	Teenage Conceptions	**Vol. 205**	Nutrition and Diet
Vol. 183	Work and Employment	**Vol. 206**	Coping with Stress
Vol. 184	Understanding Eating Disorders	**Vol. 207**	Consumerism and Ethics
Vol. 185	Student Matters	**Vol. 208**	Genetic Modification
Vol. 186	Cannabis Use	**Vol. 209**	Education and Society
Vol. 187	Health and the State	**Vol. 210**	The Media
Vol. 188	Tobacco and Health	**Vol. 211**	Biotechnology and Cloning

Vol. 212	International Terrorism
Vol. 213	The Armed Forces
Vol. 214	Vegetarian Diets
Vol. 215	Religion in Society
Vol. 216	Tackling Climate Change
Vol. 217	Euthanasia and Assisted Suicide
Vol. 218	A Sustainable Future
Vol. 219	Class and Social Mobility
Vol. 220	Population Growth and Migration
Vol. 221	Equality and Gender Roles
Vol. 222	Tourism and Travel
Vol. 223	Crime. Punishment and Justice
Vol. 224	Domestic and Relationship Abuse
Vol. 225	LGBT Equality
Vol. 226	Globalisation and Trade
Vol. 227	Ethics in Business
Vol. 228	Illegal Drug Use
Vol. 229	Protecting Human Rights
Vol. 230	Evolution of the Internet
Vol. 231	The Abortion Debate
Vol. 232	Bullying in our Society
Vol. 233	Exploring Animal Rights
Vol. 234	Skin Deep - debating body image
Vol. 235	The Poverty Crisis

sexualisation of young girls **174**.38-9; **221**.9-10

smacking *see* smacking

and smoking **176**.3, 12-13

   health effects **176**.12-13

   and the law **176**.13

   passive smoking **188**.5, 11

and social mobility **219**.27

and social housing **181**.9-11

and suicide **176**.35, 36-7

as suicide bombers **212**.11-12

time spent with fathers **191**.32

tobacco pickers, health problems **188**.39

toy preferences and gender **221**.7-8

travel to school **200**.1-2, 19-20

undernourishment, developing countries **235**.26-7

and vegetarian diet **214**.28, 36

viewing Internet pornography **196**.38

and women's careers **183**.21

of working mothers **221**.26

see also boys and young men; girls and young women;
   young people

Children's Act and divorce **166**.34

children's rights **229**.24-6

  and corporal punishment **179**.30, 31-2

  to education **229**.24, 27-8

  UK **229**.29-30

  UN Convention on the Rights of the Child **229**.24-6

chimeras (human-animal hybrids)

  for stem cell research **178**.35

China

  child labour **202**.11

  death penalty **229**.37

  economic development **226**.21

  Google withdrawing from China **196**.27-28, 29, 30

  one-child rule **220**.4, 18

  patriotic hacking **196**.34-5

  population trends **220**.8

  poverty rates **235**.23

  receiving waste from UK **161**.17

  straddling bus **200**.29

Chinese medicine, risks **195**.36

chlamydia **173**.17, 20; **176**.25, 26

  online testing for **173**.28

chlorinating water, environmental impact **218**.38-9

chocolate, labelling rules **205**.12

Choosing to Die documentary **217**.20

Christianity **215**.1-2

  and abortion **231**.19

  and Britain **215**.14

  as default religion in Britain **215**.15-16

  and equality legislation **215**.25

  funerals **192**.34

  and the law **215**.26-7

  and vegetarianism **214**.6

church attendance **215**.6

cigar smoking **188**.3

cigarettes

  chemicals in **188**.4, 9-10, 15

  consumption statistics **188**.3

  cost **188**.15, 22

  health warnings on packs ineffective **188**.29

  packaging giving misleading messages **188**.20

  see also smoking

Cinematograph Films (Animals) Act **196**.14

CIRA (Continuity IRA) **212**.14

circles of support, for sex offenders **179**.22-3

circuses, use of wild animals **233**.4, 14-15

CITES (Convention on International Trade in Endangered
Species) **193**.2

cities *see* cars, congestion; urban areas; urban growth

citizenship **175**.1, 8

  ceremonies for 18 year olds **175**.13-15

  definition **175**.1, 32

  and Muslims **215**.9-10

  survey **175**.6-7

  tests **175**.15; **220**.30-31

  and young people **175**.30-32; 38-9

citizenship education **175**.1, 37

  effects of **175**.38-9

  young people's attitudes to **175**.32, 37

civil marriage ceremonies **166**.6; **191**.3

civil partnerships

  dissolution **166**.21-2

  legal equivalence with marriage **225**.35

  for opposite-sex couples **225**.33

  in religious buildings **225**.32

civil rights on surveillance **168**.10

civil servants **175**.20

class *see* social class

classification

  of drugs **186**.32-3; **228**.21, 24, 25

   criticism of **228**.22-3

   designer drugs **228**.32-3

   effect on policing **186**.36-7

   reclassification of cannabis **186**.4-5, 31, 32; **228**.23

  of films **196**.13-16

  of video games **196**.17

climate change **193**.5; **216**.1-39; **218**.19

  adaptation to **216**.28, 29-30

  and British weather **216**.4, 8, 9

  Cancun Agreement **226**.4

  controversies **216**.18-27

  definitions **216**.5

  effects of **216**.4, 6-7, 8, 9, 10-12, 14

  evidence for **216**.3, 5-6, 18-19, 20, 22-4

  and food production **205**.30; **214**.17, 18, 19, 21;
216.6-7, 10

  and forests **216**.14-15

  and Galapagos Islands **193**.24-5

  international agreements **216**.37-9; **226**.4

  measurement **216**.26-7

  and meat production **214**.17, 18, 19, 21

  mechanisms **216**.2

  and migration **220**.20, 28, 29

  mitigation **216**.7, 28

  political attitudes **216**.25

  predictions **216**.6, 9

  public attitudes **216**.21, 24, 25, 32; **218**.14

  refugees **216**.10-11

  and renewable energy sources

   microgeneration **204**.36

   wind energy **204**.12

response to **216**.28-39
scepticism **216**.23-4, 25
and sea level **216**.9, 16-17, 20-21
and tourism **222**.22
UN rainforest protection initiative **218**.20-21
and water resources **218**.33
and whales and dolphins **193**.29
see also energy efficiency; global warming; greenhouse
gas emissions
climate events of 2010 **216**.13
climate forcing **216**.1
climate justice **218**.4
climate measurement **216**.26-7
climate models **216**.2
climate sensitivity **216**.2
clinical (major) depression **190**.2, 21
cloning *see* animal cloning; human cloning
clostridium difficile **187**.28, 29
clothes
as economic indicator **180**.5
energy-harvesting **204**.39
recycling **161**.28
clubs and societies at university **185**.6-7
CO₂ *see* carbon dioxide
co-parenting, same-sex couples **178**.9
coach travel, disabled people **197**.12
coal, production trends **204**.1
coastal areas
effect of climate change **216**.7
effects of tourism **222**.25
coat of arms, Royal **175**.2
cocoa, labelling rules **205**.12
coercive control and domestic violence **224**.34-5
coffee
and hydration **205**.27
labelling rules **205**.12
Cognitive Behavioural Therapy (CBT)
and eating disorders **184**.37-8
and phobias **206**.13
and post traumatic stress disorder, armed forces **213**.34
and problem gambling **203**.24

and stress **206**.3, 12
cognitive therapy for depression **190**.34
cohabitation **166**.1, 12, 14-15
and expectation of marriage **166**.2, 7
legal rights **166**.12, 14-15
cold weather payments **204**.23
Cole, Cheryl, and cyberbullying **232**.38
Colombia, town banning tourists **222**.32
colorants, food **205**.14-15
colour preferences and gender **221**.7-8
combined heat and power (CHP)
and fuel cells **204**.38
microgeneration **204**.35
comedy and racism **172**.11-12
commercial radio **210**.3
commercial sexual exploitation of children **202**.16-31
definition **202**.16
commercialisation, effect on children **207**.38-9
committees, Parliamentary **175**.35-6
commodification of children **178**.12
Common Agricultural Policy, impact on developing
countries **226**.33
'common law' marriages **166**.12
communication
needs of disabled children **197**.37
trends **210**.4-5
see also media; telecommunications; telephones
communications data **168**.8, 13-14, 32-3
government database **168**.13-14
privacy **168**.2
community cohesion **175**.6-7
community disclosure of sex offenders **179**.20-21
Community Self Build **181**.30-31
community sentences **223**.20, 23
company boards *see* boardroom positions
Compassion in Dying information line **217**.37
compensation and the Human Rights Act **229**.5-6
competitive sport in schools **198**.5

complementary and alternative medicine (CAM)
195.1-39

Vol. numbers appear first (in bold) followed by page numbers; a change in volume is preceded by a semi-**colon.**

Vol. 159	An Ageing Population	**Vol. 189**	The Homeless Population	**Vol. 212**	International Terrorism
Vol. 161	Waste Issues	**Vol. 190**	Coping with Depression	**Vol. 213**	The Armed Forces
Vol. 162	Staying Fit	**Vol. 191**	The Changing Family	**Vol. 214**	Vegetarian Diets
Vol. 164	The AIDS Crisis	**Vol. 192**	Bereavement and Grief	**Vol. 215**	Religion in Society
Vol. 166	Marriage and Cohabitation	**Vol. 193**	Endangered Species	**Vol. 216**	Tackling Climate Change
Vol. 168	Privacy and Surveillance	**Vol. 194**	Responsible Drinking	**Vol. 217**	Euthanasia and Assisted Suicide
Vol. 172	Racial and Ethnic Discrimination	**Vol. 195**	Alternative Medicine	**Vol. 218**	A Sustainable Future
Vol. 173	Sexual Health	**Vol. 196**	Censorship Issues	**Vol. 219**	Class and Social Mobility
Vol. 174	Selling Sex	**Vol. 197**	Living with Disability	**Vol. 220**	Population Growth and Migration
Vol. 175	Citizenship and Participation	**Vol. 198**	Sport and Society	**Vol. 221**	Equality and Gender Roles
Vol. 176	Health Issues for Young People	**Vol. 199**	Self-Harming and Suicide	**Vol. 222**	Tourism and Travel
Vol. 177	Crime in the UK	**Vol. 200**	Sustainable Transport	**Vol. 223**	Crime. Punishment and Justice
Vol. 178	Reproductive Ethics	**Vol. 201**	Mental Wellbeing	**Vol. 224**	Domestic and Relationship Abuse
Vol. 179	Tackling Child Abuse	**Vol. 202**	Child Exploitation	**Vol. 225**	LGBT Equality
Vol. 180	Money and Finances	**Vol. 203**	The Gambling Problem	**Vol. 226**	Globalisation and Trade
Vol. 181	The Housing Issue	**Vol. 204**	The Energy Crisis	**Vol. 227**	Ethics in Business
Vol. 182	Teenage Conceptions	**Vol. 205**	Nutrition and Diet	**Vol. 228**	Illegal Drug Use
Vol. 183	Work and Employment	**Vol. 206**	Coping with Stress	**Vol. 229**	Protecting Human Rights
Vol. 184	Understanding Eating Disorders	**Vol. 207**	Consumerism and Ethics	**Vol. 230**	Evolution of the Internet
Vol. 185	Student Matters	**Vol. 208**	Genetic Modification	**Vol. 231**	The Abortion Debate
Vol. 186	Cannabis Use	**Vol. 209**	Education and Society	**Vol. 232**	Bullying in our Society
Vol. 187	Health and the State	**Vol. 210**	The Media	**Vol. 233**	Exploring Animal Rights
Vol. 188	Tobacco and Health	**Vol. 211**	Biotechnology and Cloning	**Vol. 234**	Skin Deep - debating body image
				Vol. 235	The Poverty Crisis

arguments against **195**.14-15
definitions **195**.1, 9
and depression **190**.11
how it works **195**.2
need for research **195**.13
popularity **195**.3
positive effects **195**.6-7
reasons for using **195**.5, 6-7
safety **195**.2
therapists **195**.1, 3
types **195**.3
see also Chinese medicine; herbal medicine; homeopathy
complementary therapies and depression **190**.11
complicated bereavement **192**.16-17
composting waste **161**.19, 28-9, 30; **218**.11-12
gas production **204**.24
comprehensive school pupils, degree performance **209**.12; **219**.32
compressed air energy storage (CAES) **204**.37-8
compulsive eating **184**.7
compulsive exercise **162**.39; **184**.7
compulsive gambling *see* problem gambling
compulsive over-eating **184**.7
compulsive shopping **207**.6
compulsory voting **175**.28-9
computer network attacks **196**.34
computers
recycling **161**.29
see also Internet
concentrating solar thermal power (CSP) **204**.3
conception **178**.2-3; **182**.3-4
rate, young people **173**.3; **182**.3
conciliation (mediation) **166**.26, 35, 38-9
concurrent sentences **223**.19
condoms **173**.2, 24; **176**.27; **182**.19, 20
and HIV **164**.3
and the prevention of STIs **173**.24
safe use **173**.5, 26
usage **164**.26; **173**.22
conflict *see* war
conflict-induced displacement **220**.36-7
conflict minerals **226**.3
congestion, traffic
London Congestion Charge **200**.17-18
public attitudes **200**.5-6
Congo
child soldiers **202**.37-9
logging industry and wildlife **193**.4
natural resources and violence **226**.3
consecutive sentences **223**.19
conservation *see* endangered species; extinction
constituencies, parliamentary **175**.23-4
constitution, British, and Christianity **215**.14
construction industry, waste recycling **161**.23
consumer adultery **161**.8-9
consumer power **207**.3-5
and ethical consumerism **207**.23-4
consumer rights **207**.12-22
credit card purchases **207**.12, 18
online shopping **207**.12, 13
consumer spending *see* spending

consumer trends **207**.1-11
consumerism
and children **207**.37-9
problems **207**.2
consumers
and child labour **202**.13-14
and child trafficking **202**.30
disability discrimination **197**.21, 25
and energy industry **218**.10
ethical shopping **226**.38
and food from cloned animals **211**.11, 12, 14
and GM foods **208**.29-30, 31, 33
older people **159**.19
rights *see* consumer rights
and sustainable development **226**.4
see also shopping
consumption
global **193**.3-4
inequality and population growth **220**.11-12, 14, 15
contact with children after divorce **166**.26, 37-8
contamination
of crops by GM crops **208**.24, 27
see also pollution
contextual targeting **230**.5
Continuity IRA (CIRA) **212**.14
continuous deep sedation **217**.25
contraception **173**.1, 3, 5, 25; **176**.27; **182**.3-4, 19-26
developing countries **220**.16-17
failure **173**.5
and young people **173**.9; **182**.1-2
see also condoms; family planning; pill, contraceptive
Convention on the Rights of the Child (UN) **202**.2
conversion therapy (homosexuality) **225**.17-18
cooperation, global **226**.17-19, 22-5
Copenhagen climate change summit **216**.37, 38
copycat suicides and media reporting **199**.36
copyright and the Internet **230**.30, 35-7
coral reefs **193**.5
economic value **193**.10
threats to **218**.24
coronary heart disease (CHD) *see* heart disease
coroner **192**.31
Coroners and Justice Act **196**.14
corporal punishment **179**.30-38
arguments against **179**.34-7
arguments for not criminalizing **179**.33
and children's rights **179**.30, 31-2
definition **179**.30, 34
and discipline **179**.37
effects **179**.34
government position **179**.33
and the law **179**.30
public opposition to **179**.32
and religious views **179**.36
Corporate Social Responsibility **207**.30; **226**.38; **227**.9-10, 12, 18-19
cortisol **206**.30
cosmetic surgery
desire for **234**.14-15, 19, 33
Girlguiding UK campaign **234**.34
regulation **234**.21

Vol. numbers appear first (in bold) followed by page numbers; a change in volume is preceded by a semi-**colon.**

crime **223**.1-18
   and aggressive behaviour in children **224**.23
   and alcohol **176**.15; **194**.20, 21, 29
   causes of criminal behaviour **223**.11
      rioting **223**.8, 9-10
   committed by children **223**.30-31
   crime mapping **223**.1-2
   cybercrime **230**.29
   fear of **159**.3
   and gangs **223**.6-7, 13-15
   HIV transmission as crime **164**.12-14
   and household insurance **235**.7
   knife crime **223**.5
      prevention **223**.6-7, 16-17, 34
      punishment **223**.21, 25
   levels of crime **223**.2, 3-5
   and licensing hours change **194**.21
   and mental health sufferers **201**.22
   phishing **230**.30
   reporting a crime **223**.12
   riots **223**.8-11
   and sexual exploitation **202**.22
   and slums **235**.37
   and surveillance **168**.27
   victims of *see* victims of crime
   see also fraud; victims of crime; violent crime; young offenders
Crime and Disorder Act **172**.9
crime prevention **223**.12-18
   and CCTV **168**.23-4
   gangs and youth violence **223**.7, 13-15, 35-6
   role of ex-offenders **223**.18
   and schools **223**.16-17
Criminal Justice Act **172**.9
   and hate crime **225**.31
Criminal Justice and Immigration Act **196**.14
   and pornography **174**.20, 21, 22-5
criminal justice system **223**.19-39
   and children **223**.29, 30-32
   gang injunctions **223**.35-6
   reforms **223**.24-5
   restorative justice **223**.28-9
   sentencing **223**.19-22, 23, 33
   see also prison
criminal responsibility, age of **223**.30
   reasons for raising **223**.31-2
criminalisation of homosexuality, globally **225**.39
criminals
   and the Human Rights Act **229**.5, 6
   see also prisoners
crop biotechnology *see* genetically modified (GM) crops
cross-contamination, GM crops **208**.24, 26
crossdressers **225**.19
Crown Jewels **175**.2
cruise ships, impact on environment **222**.25
cryogenic ID tags and IVF **178**.22-3
cryopreservation *see* freezing
crystal meth (methamphetamine) **228**.23
CSP (concentrating solar thermal power) **204**.3
CSS (carbon capture and storage) **204**.27
cultural identity **172**.27

British *see* British identity
   mixed-race **172**.31-3
   second generation children **172**.29
cultural traditions and death **192**.29, 34-6
culture
   and body image **234**.3
   and corporal punishment **179**.36
   and fatherhood **191**.33
   effect of tourism **222**.22, 29, 30
currency, British **175**.2
current accounts **180**.25
curriculum
   and faith schools **215**.19
   reform **209**.5
custody *see* prison; youth custody
customer service lines **207**.14
   credit card companies **207**.17-18
customs regulations on indecent articles **196**.23
cutting (self-harm)
   emergency treatment **199**.13-14
   safety measures **199**.7
cyber stalking **230**.23
cyberbullying **230**.23; **232**.2, 25-39
   dealing with **232**.3, 26, 29, 39
   effects **232**.25, 26
   forms **232**.25
   prevalence **232**.30, 31
   preventing **230**.28; **232**.26-7, 28
   reasons for **232**.25-6
   reporting **232**.29
   at work **227**.38
cybercrime **230**.29
cycling **200**.21
   cycles sharing roads with cars **200**.18
   impact of traffic **200**.16
   to school **200**.1-2
cyclothymia **190**.9; **201**.15

D

dairy farming, mega-dairies **233**.9-10
dairy foods *see* milk; milk products
Dangerous Dogs Act **233**.4, 12-13
dark tourism **222**.16
data protection
   personal protection measures **168**.31-2, 37
   and self-regulation **168**.2
Data Protection Act **168**.10-11, 31, 37
date rape drugs **194**.8-10
dead zones, oceans **218**.24-5
death penalty **223**.37-9; **229**.37-8
   and European Court of Human Rights **229**.39
deaths
   alcohol-related **194**.13
   in Armed Forces **213**.9
   of children **192**.20-23
   children's understanding of death **192**.4, 13, 15, 19
   discussing own wishes about dying **192**.8, 24
   drug-related **228**.2, 13

earlier death of mental health sufferers **201**.26
funerals **192**.30-31, 34-7
older people, winter **159**.4
practical matters **192**.24, 29-33
registering **192**.29-30
see also bereavement; euthanasia
debates, Parliamentary **175**.18, 19
Debenhams, using disabled model **197**.10
DeBique, Tilern **213**.13-14
debit cards **180**.13, 26
debt **180**.9-12
advice **180**.27
affecting more affluent people **180**.10
buying on credit **207**.6, 16
developing world **226**.5-6
increasing incidence of debt **180**.11
need for education about debt **180**.38
statistics **180**.9, 10, 11, 12
students **185**.12-13, 17; **209**.31-2
debt cancellation, developing countries **226**.5-6
debt crisis **180**.10-12; **226**.5
Declaration of Internet Freedom **230**.37
decree absolute **166**.22, 26
decree nisi **166**.22, 26
decriminalisation of drugs possession **228**.34
default retirement age **183**.14-15
defence
budget cuts **213**.17-19, 20-21, 22-3, 28
see also Armed Forces
deforestation
and cattle ranching **193**.14
dryland forests **218**.21
and palm oil industry **193**.14
rainforest protection programme **218**.20-21
degrees, university
costs **185**.11, 17
courses **185**.5-6
and earnings **185**.21, 32-4
for nurses **187**.33-5
and students' school background **209**.12; **219**.32
dementia **159**.4, 35-9

and depression **201**.12-13
fear of **159**.39
in younger people **201**.10-11
see also Alzheimer's disease
dementia services **201**.5, 10-11
democracy
and Islam **215**.10
see also elections
demographic transition **220**.3
demographics *see* population; population growth
demonstrations via the Internet **196**.32
dependency, on alcohol **194**.6, 15
depressant drugs (downers) **228**.3
see also cannabis; heroin; solvents
depression **190**.1-39
anti-depressant drugs *see* anti-depressant drugs
and cannabis use **186**.10
causes of **190**.2-3, 4, 5
in children and young people **176**.30, 32
and complementary therapies **190**.11
definitions **190**.21-2
and dementia **201**.12-13
and desire for success **190**.13
diagnosis
bipolar disorder **190**.8
GPs difficulty diagnosing depression **190**.31
teenage depression **190**.25-6
and exercise **162**.37, 38, **190**.3, 38
genetic factors **190**.2, 4, 11, 12-13
manic depression *see* bipolar affective disorder
and meditation **190**.34-6; **195**.15
and men **190**.18-19
and mortality **190**.20
and physical illness **190**.3, 5
post-natal **190**.2, 14-17, 21-2
prevalence of **190**.22-3, 30
and redundancy **183**.11
statistics **190**.7, 27, 30
students **185**.8
and suicide **190**.21, 23-4
young people **190**.26-7

Vol. numbers appear first (in bold) followed by page numbers; a change in volume is preceded by a semi-**colon.**

Vol. 159	An Ageing Population
Vol. 161	Waste Issues
Vol. 162	Staying Fit
Vol. 164	The AIDS Crisis
Vol. 166	Marriage and Cohabitation
Vol. 168	Privacy and Surveillance
Vol. 172	Racial and Ethnic Discrimination
Vol. 173	Sexual Health
Vol. 174	Selling Sex
Vol. 175	Citizenship and Participation
Vol. 176	Health Issues for Young People
Vol. 177	Crime in the UK
Vol. 178	Reproductive Ethics
Vol. 179	Tackling Child Abuse
Vol. 180	Money and Finances
Vol. 181	The Housing Issue
Vol. 182	Teenage Conceptions
Vol. 183	Work and Employment
Vol. 184	Understanding Eating Disorders
Vol. 185	Student Matters
Vol. 186	Cannabis Use
Vol. 187	Health and the State
Vol. 188	Tobacco and Health
Vol. 189	The Homeless Population
Vol. 190	Coping with Depression
Vol. 191	The Changing Family
Vol. 192	Bereavement and Grief
Vol. 193	Endangered Species
Vol. 194	Responsible Drinking
Vol. 195	Alternative Medicine
Vol. 196	Censorship Issues
Vol. 197	Living with Disability
Vol. 198	Sport and Society
Vol. 199	Self-Harming and Suicide
Vol. 200	Sustainable Transport
Vol. 201	Mental Wellbeing
Vol. 202	Child Exploitation
Vol. 203	The Gambling Problem
Vol. 204	The Energy Crisis
Vol. 205	Nutrition and Diet
Vol. 206	Coping with Stress
Vol. 207	Consumerism and Ethics
Vol. 208	Genetic Modification
Vol. 209	Education and Society
Vol. 210	The Media
Vol. 211	Biotechnology and Cloning
Vol. 212	International Terrorism
Vol. 213	The Armed Forces
Vol. 214	Vegetarian Diets
Vol. 215	Religion in Society
Vol. 216	Tackling Climate Change
Vol. 217	Euthanasia and Assisted Suicide
Vol. 218	A Sustainable Future
Vol. 219	Class and Social Mobility
Vol. 220	Population Growth and Migration
Vol. 221	Equality and Gender Roles
Vol. 222	Tourism and Travel
Vol. 223	Crime, Punishment and Justice
Vol. 224	Domestic and Relationship Abuse
Vol. 225	LGBT Equality
Vol. 226	Globalisation and Trade
Vol. 227	Ethics in Business
Vol. 228	Illegal Drug Use
Vol. 229	Protecting Human Rights
Vol. 230	Evolution of the Internet
Vol. 231	The Abortion Debate
Vol. 232	Bullying in our Society
Vol. 233	Exploring Animal Rights
Vol. 234	Skin Deep - debating body image
Vol. 235	The Poverty Crisis

symptoms **190**.1-2; 21, 22; **199**.29
   bipolar disorder **190**.8-9, 21
   post-natal depression **190**.14
   seasonal affective disorder **190**.6
   young people **190**.26
treatments **190**.31-9
   drugs **190**.10-11, 26, 32-3
   see also anti-depressant drugs
   manic depression **190**.10-11
   psychotherapy **190**.5, 11, 34, 37
   Seasonal Affective Disorder **190**.6-7
   self-help **190**.38-9
   young people **190**.25
types of **190**.2, 21-2
unipolar (endogenous) **190**.10
young people **176**.30, 32; **190**.25-30
   and university **176**.6
see also bipolar affective disorder, (manic depression);
   seasonal affective disorder (SAD)
designer babies **178**.31-2
designer drugs, control of **228**.32-3
desoxypipradol **228**.25, 37
detention of terrorist suspects **212**.16
determinate sentences **223**.19-20
detox diets **205**.22
developed countries, impact of globalization **226**.24-5
developing countries
   age structures **220**.8
   ageing populations **159**.5
   aid to *see* aid
   and AIDS/HIV **164**.10
   biofuels causing food shortages **204**.33-4
   child labour **202**.9-12
   and climate change **216**.11
   and contraception **220**.16-17
   damaging effects of recycling **161**.35
   dangers of homeopathy **195**.30-31
   debt **226**.5-6
   definition **226**.30
   education **209**.8; **229**.27-8
   fertility rates **220**.2, 3, 4, 12, 13
   and free trade **226**.32, 33-4
   gender inequality **221**.1-2, 35
   girls' education **221**.35, 38-9; **229**.27-8
   and globalisation **226**.3-4
   and GM crops **208**.10
   and ICT **230**.7
   loans for small businesses **235**.33-5
   pensions **159**.24
   and population growth **220**.2, 4, 5-7
   and poverty **235**.23-39
   poverty reduction strategies **235**.24
   receiving unwanted waste **161**.37
   remittances from migrant workers **220**.35
   and renewable energy **204**.2
   slum tourism **222**.16, 33-4
   and transport **200**.13
   UK trade initiatives **226**.28
   World Bank support **226**.9-10
   and World Trade Organization **226**.8
   see also Millennium Development Development Goals

development-induced displacement **220**.37
devolved Government **175**.17
diabetes and meat consumption **214**.35
diet
   healthy *see* healthy eating
   importance of breakfast **205**.8-9
   macrobiotic **195**.4-5
   and mental health **190**.3
   and stress **206**.33
   and weight loss **162**.2
   worldwide changes **162**.6
   UK population **205**.1, 17
   young people **176**.8-9
   see also dieting; eating disorders; food and nutrition;
healthy
     eating; veganism; vegetarianism
diet industry **234**.7-8
dietary obsession (orthorexia nervosa) **184**.9
dietary supplements **205**.4
   and vegetarian diet **214**.10, 29
dieting **205**.22-3
   and body image **234**.12
   mothers, effects on daughters **184**.21-2
   teenage girls **184**.22
digital dating abuse **224**.20
digital fluency **230**.10-12
digital footprints **230**.31-2
digital literacy **230**.13
digital natives **230**.8-9
digital radio **210**.15
Dignity in Dying **217**.38
   criticism of assisted suicide policy **217**.26
dilation and evacuation (abortion) **231**.7
diplomas, gender-stereotypical choices **221**.28
direct debits **180**.14
direct discrimination
  racial **172**.4, 17
   sexual orientation **225**.28
directors, company *see* boardroom positions
disability
   and abortion **231**.20
   acceptable language **197**.27
   benefits **197**.31-4
   definitions **197**.1-2
   discrimination **197**.20-23
     in healthcare **197**.30-31, 38-9
     workplace **197**.20-21
     see also Disability Discrimination Act
   and employment **197**.20-21, 24-5, 26-7
   hidden disabilities **197**.8
   learning disabilities **197**.6-7
   and mental health, young people **201**.3
   physical disabilities **197**.3-5
   and poverty **197**.35
   and transport **197**.11-12, 23
   see also disabled children; disabled people
Disability Discrimination Act **197**.8-9, 24-5
   and workplace stress **206**.28
Disability Living Allowance **197**.31-4
disability rights
   access to goods and services **197**.21, 25

education 197.22-3
housing 197.21-2
transport 197.11-12, 23
at work 197.20-21, 24-5, 26-7
disabled children
learning disabilities 197.14-15
needs 197.36-7
physical disabilities 197.3-5
siblings of disabled children 197.18-19
disabled people
and assisted suicide 199.39; 217.19, 21
benefit cuts 229.32
discrimination 197.20-23, 30-31, 38-9
see also Disability discrimination Act
and domestic abuse 224.4
and employment 197.20-21, 24-5, 26-7
in low-income households 235.5, 7
model used in advertising campaign 197.10
and sport 198.18, 20-21
and transport 197.11-12, 23
see also disability; learning disabilities
disablism see discrimination, disabled people
disaster-induced displacement 220.37
disaster tourism 222.16
disaster victims, older people 159.6
discipline
role of fathers 191.31-2
see also corporal punishment; smacking
DISCO, EU biofuels project 204.32
discretionary eviction 181.16
discrimination
anti-discrimination legislation 183.13; 221.3, 36
and workplace stress 206.28-9
and child trafficking 202.28
against Christians 215.25
definition 221.3
disabled people 197.20-23
in healthcare 197.30-31, 38-9
at work 197.20-21
see also Disability Discrimination Act
gender discrimination at work 221.18, 23-4

see also gender pay gap
against Muslims 215.30, 31-2
and obesity 162.21
racial see racial discrimination
religious 215.23-4; 30; 31-2
sexual orientation 225.9-10, 28-9
and religious beliefs 225.35
in the workplace 197.20-21; 215.23-4; 221.18, 23-4
see also prejudice; racism; sex discrimination
disease
resistance, GM crops 208.1, 29
stem cell treatment 211.30, 36-7, 38-9
displaced people see refugees
disposable nappies, waste 161.1, 5, 29
dispute settlement, World Trade Organization 226.8
dissociation, prostitutes 174.5
distraction techniques, self-harmers 199.5-6, 8
diuretics as banned substances in sport 198.29
diversity in Parliament 175.21
divorce 166.3, 21-39
and children 166.4-5, 29-31, 32, 34-8; 191.1, 9
and children's mental health 201.3
and duration of marriage 166.27, 28
emotional effects 166.22-4
how to help 166.24
legal process 166.22
reasons for 166.21-2
risk factors 166.28
statistics 166.3, 4, 6, 25, 27, 28; 191.1, 8
DNA 168.7, 11-12; 208.7; 211.3
damage by cannabis use 186.14
DNA database 168.7, 11-12
Do Not Attempt Resuscitation (DNAR) order 217.3, 14
docking dogs' tails 233.6
doctors
and abortion 231.2, 25, 28, 29, 32-3
asking about patient's alcohol consumption 194.33, 37-8
and assisted suicide 217.4, 8, 11, 22, 24-5, 31
GP patient survey 187.16-17
and help for eating disorders 184.36

Vol. numbers appear first (in bold) followed by page numbers; a change in volume is preceded by a semi-colon.

Vol. 159 An Ageing Population
Vol. 161 Waste Issues
Vol. 162 Staying Fit
Vol. 164 The AIDS Crisis
Vol. 166 Marriage and Cohabitation
Vol. 168 Privacy and Surveillance
Vol. 172 Racial and Ethnic Discrimination
Vol. 173 Sexual Health
Vol. 174 Selling Sex
Vol. 175 Citizenship and Participation
Vol. 176 Health Issues for Young People
Vol. 177 Crime in the UK
Vol. 178 Reproductive Ethics
Vol. 179 Tackling Child Abuse
Vol. 180 Money and Finances
Vol. 181 The Housing Issue
Vol. 182 Teenage Conceptions
Vol. 183 Work and Employment
Vol. 184 Understanding Eating Disorders
Vol. 185 Student Matters
Vol. 186 Cannabis Use
Vol. 187 Health and the State
Vol. 188 Tobacco and Health

Vol. 189 The Homeless Population
Vol. 190 Coping with Depression
Vol. 191 The Changing Family
Vol. 192 Bereavement and Grief
Vol. 193 Endangered Species
Vol. 194 Responsible Drinking
Vol. 195 Alternative Medicine
Vol. 196 Censorship Issues
Vol. 197 Living with Disability
Vol. 198 Sport and Society
Vol. 199 Self-Harming and Suicide
Vol. 200 Sustainable Transport
Vol. 201 Mental Wellbeing
Vol. 202 Child Exploitation
Vol. 203 The Gambling Problem
Vol. 204 The Energy Crisis
Vol. 205 Nutrition and Diet
Vol. 206 Coping with Stress
Vol. 207 Consumerism and Ethics
Vol. 208 Genetic Modification
Vol. 209 Education and Society
Vol. 210 The Media
Vol. 211 Biotechnology and Cloning

Vol. 212 International Terrorism
Vol. 213 The Armed Forces
Vol. 214 Vegetarian Diets
Vol. 215 Religion in Society
Vol. 216 Tackling Climate Change
Vol. 217 Euthanasia and Assisted Suicide
Vol. 218 A Sustainable Future
Vol. 219 Class and Social Mobility
Vol. 220 Population Growth and Migration
Vol. 221 Equality and Gender Roles
Vol. 222 Tourism and Travel
Vol. 223 Crime. Punishment and Justice
Vol. 224 Domestic and Relationship Abuse
Vol. 225 LGBT Equality
Vol. 226 Globalisation and Trade
Vol. 227 Ethics in Business
Vol. 228 Illegal Drug Use
Vol. 229 Protecting Human Rights
Vol. 230 Evolution of the Internet
Vol. 231 The Abortion Debate
Vol. 232 Bullying in our Society
Vol. 233 Exploring Animal Rights
Vol. 234 Skin Deep - debating body image
Vol. 235 The Poverty Crisis

relationship with patients **187**.31
    impact of legalizing assisted dying **217**.4, 8, 11, 31
role in NHS **187**.25, 26
trusted by the public **187**.18
see also GPs (general practitioners); physician-assisted
    suicide (PAS)
doctrine of double effect **217**.5, 14
Dog Control Bill **233**.4
dogs
    and animal rights **233**.4
    Dangerous Dogs Act **233**.4, 12-13
    tail docking **233**.6
Dolly the sheep **211**.7, 8
dolphins
    dolphin-watching holidays **222**.26
    impact of climate change **193**.29
    rights **233**.20
domestic abuse **224**.1-39
    children **189**.27
    costs **224**.27
    definitions **224**.1, 34-7
    excuses for **224**.1-2
    help for perpetrators **224**.39
    help for victims **224**.38
    impact on children **224**.24-6, 37
    lesbian, gay ,bisexual and transgender
        relationships **224**.5, 12-13
    male victims **224**.5, 9-10, 11
    and mental health of children **201**.3
    myths **224**.6-7
    personal stories **224**.8, 21, 26
    prevalence of **224**.28
    prevention strategy **224**.28-31
    signs of abuse
        in children **224**.24, 25
        in teenagers **224**.16-17
    statistics **224**.11
    staying with an abusive partner **224**.6
    support for victims **224**.38
    and young people **179**.19; **224**.4, 16-26
domestic waste *see* household waste
domestic workers
    children **202**.12
    and human trafficking **229**.18
donor insemination **178**.9
donors, eggs and sperm
    contact with offspring **178**.25, 26-7
    donor anonymity **178**.11, 24
    numbers falling **178**.24
'don't ask don't tell' policy, US military **225**.38-9
doping *see* drugs in sport
Dove, self-esteem campaign **234**.33
downers *see* depressant drugs
downshifting **183**.18
drag queens/kings **225**.19
Drax power plant, biomass fuel **204**.5, 7
drink-driving **194**.31
    reducing alcohol limit **194**.32
drink spiking **194**.8-10
drinking water access **218**.31-3, 36
driving

and alcohol *see* drink-driving
and cannabis use **186**.10
dementia sufferers **201**.11
and disabled people **197**.11
driving licences, EU **168**.9
motorway phobia **200**.4
drought **218**.23
drug abuse **176**.6, 19; **228**.1-39
    and beggars **189**.35-6
    costs **228**.1-2, 24
    deaths from **228**.2, 13
    declining **228**.35
    drug education campaign **228**.10-11
    effects **228**.12-13
    and fertility **178**.4, 5
    and HIV **164**.17, 25
    and homeless people **189**.10, 13, 35-6
    ketamine **228**.5
    legal highs **228**.1, 36-8
    and sex **173**.15
    signs of **228**.14-15
    and smoking **176**.12
    statistics **176**.18; **228**.1, 13, 35
    students **185**.8, 9
    treatment **228**.16-18
    trends **228**.1
    types of drugs **228**.3-4
    worldwide **186**.18-21
    young people **176**.6, 18
    see also cannabis
drug gangs, targeted by National Crime Agency **223**.22
drug overdoses, emergency treatment **199**.14; **228**.2
drug policy **228**.24-7
    and designer drugs **228**.32-3
    need for review **228**.39
    see also classification of drugs
drug testing
    in sport **198**.27, 28
        punishment for missing tests **198**.39
    at work **168**.38
drug treatments
    for depression **190**.32-3
        for bipolar disorder **190**.10-11
        as cause of depression **190**.3
        and teenage depression **190**.26
        see also anti-depressants
    for gambling addiction **203**.27
drugs
    animal research in drug development **233**.30-33
    assessment of drug harms **186**.33
    assessment for NHS use **187**.22-3
    for assisted dying, availability **217**.34
    cannabis *see* cannabis
    classification **228**.21, 24, 25
        cannabis **186**.4-5, 31, 32-3; 23
        criticism of **228**.22-3
    date rape drugs **194**.8-10
    decriminalisation campaign **228**.34
    definition **228**.21
    effects **228**.4, 12-20
        cannabis **186**.1-29

and fertility **178**.4, 5
global illicit drugs problem **186**.20-21
government policies **186**.35-6; **228**.24-7
and the law **176**.19; **228**.21-39; **228**.13, 21-39
patients' rights under NHS **187**.14
and politics **186**.34-6
types **228**.3-4
for weight loss **162**.2-3, 6, 20
see also drug abuse; medicines
drugs in sport **198**.27-39
anabolic steroids **198**.29-30
analgesics **198**.28-9
arguments for and against **198**.33-7
dangers **198**.34
diuretics **198**.29
drug testing **198**.27, 28, 39
history of **198**.32
hormones **198**.29-30
reasons for taking drugs **198**.28, 32
stimulants **198**.29
therapeutic use exemption **198**.28
drunkorexia **184**.16
dryland forests **218**.21
dual diagnosis **201**.9, 17
homeless people **189**.10-11
dumping (trade) **226**.30, 32
dysthymia **190**.10, 21, 23

E

e-cigarettes **188**.21
E.coli **187**.28
E-number food additives **205**.14
early marriage **202**.19
early onset dementia **201**.10-11
early years education *see* foundation stage education
earnings
attitudes to wage levels **219**.15
footballers **198**.11-12

gender gap *see* gender pay gap
graduates **183**.34; **185**.32-4
and university status **185**.21
minimum wage, young workers **183**.28
see also incomes; salaries; wages
Eastern European migrants, UK **220**.24-5
eating disorders **176**.9, 30, 39; **184**.1-16
causes **184**.2, 4, 5, 6, 28
and compulsive exercise **162**.39
effects **184**.1-2
getting help **184**.2, 29-39
risk factors **184**.2, 13
students **185**.8
teenagers **184**.21-2, 30-31
and going to university **176**.6
see also anorexia nervosa; bulimia nervosa; obesity
eating habits
students **209**.32, 33
see also diet; healthy eating
eco-housing **216**.29-30
eco-lodges **222**.24
economic (financial) abuse **224**.3
economic growth
Brazil **226**.20-21
China **226**.21
and globalisation **226**.3-4
and higher education **183**.34
impact of climate change **216**.11-12
impact of population growth **220**.7
indicators of recovery **180**.5
need for international cooperation **226**.17-19
role of business **227**.14
economy
global, and biodiversity **193**.10-12
recession **180**.1-5
impact on abortion rate **231**.13
and tobacco **188**.22-3
and tourism **222**.28, 30
Britain **222**.4-5
ecosystems
biodiversity **218**.18

impact of climate change **216**.6
ecotourism **222**.8-9, 22-3, 24-5, 27-8
eco-towns **181**.36-9
ecstasy (MDMA), signs of use **228**.14
ECT (electro-convulsive therapy) **190**.11
Ecuador, compulsory voting **175**.29
ED-NOS (eating disorder not otherwise specified) **184**.7-8
EDCs (endocrine disrupting chemicals) **193**.16-17
Editor's Code (Press Complaints Commission) **210**.27-8
education **209**.1-39
    and alcohol **194**.20
    and body image **234**.11, 21, 29-30
    and the Budget **180**.24
    effects of cannabis use **186**.9-10
    and child labour **202**.4-5, 14
    and child poverty **235**.21-2
    and child trafficking **202**.28
    children's rights **229**.24-5
    citizenship **175**.1, 8, 32, 37, 38-9
    in developing countries **209**.8; **229**.27-8
    and disabled children **197**.14-15, 22-3, 37
    on drugs, campaign for **228**.10-11
    early years, and social mobility **219**.17-18, 34-5
    faith-based schools **215**.17-22
    financial **180**.36-9
    girls
        barriers to education **221**.35, 38-9
        and population control **220**.7
    global gender inequality **221**.1, 35
    higher education *see* higher education; universities
    about HIV **164**.18, 23-4
    ICT skills **230**.13
    international comparisons **183**.34
    and learning disabilities **197**.14-15
    Millennium Development Goals **218**.39; **229**.27-8
    and multiculturalism **172**.36-7
    and poverty **202**.4; **235**.21-2
    racial differences **172**.14-16
    and relationship abuse **224**.17
    single-sex schools **221**.30-32
    and social mobility **219**.17-18, 22, 23, 25-6, 27-8, 34-5
    special educational needs (SEN) **197**.14-15, 23
    and teenage pregnancy **182**.31
    see also educational achievement; schools; sex education;
students; teachers; universities
Education and Inspection Act 2006 **225**.7
educational achievement
    and bullying **232**.8
    and child poverty **235**.21
    degree level, and school background **209**.12; **219**.32
    and environmental behaviour **218**.9
    and parental support **219**.33
    and socio-economic background **209**.13-14; **219**.22, 23,
25-6, 27-8, 29-30, 34
    standards improving **209**.7-10
    statistics **235**.6
    terrorist suspects **212**.9
    white British pupils, effect of social class **219**.29-30
    see also exam results
educational aspirations and race discrimination

172.15,16
Educational Maintenance Allowance (EMA) **182**.6;
    209.17, 18
EEA (European Environment Agency) **200**.22
egg donation **178**.10-12
    for embryonic stem cell research **178**.34-5
    numbers declining **178**.24
    for research cloning **211**.30
    risks **178**.12
egg freezing **178**.23
eggs and vegetarian diets **214**.2
Egypt, girls' education **229**.27-8
Ehrlich, Paul **220**.11
ejaculation **178**.3
    disorders **178**.5
elderly people
    and dementia *see* dementia
    elder abuse **159**.4, 6, 16-18; **224**.4
    and suicide **199**.20, 21
    see also ageing population; grandparents; older people
elections **175**.22-5
    compulsory voting **175**.28-9
    increasing voter turnout **175**.26-7
    terminology **175**.26
electoral register **175**.23, 26
electoral systems **175**.24-5
electric buses **200**.28-9
electric cars **200**.26, 27; **204**.7
electricity markets, Europe **204**.11-12
electro-convulsive therapy (ECT) **190**.11
electronic cigarettes **188**.21
electronic equipment recycling **161**.8-9, 23-4
electronic waste, illegal trade **218**.15-16
elephants, as endangered species **193**.2, 19
elevated water storage **204**.38
ELVs, recycling **161**.23
EMA (Educational Maintenance Allowance) **182**.6;
    209.17, 18
email
    and bullying **232**.25
    security **232**.27
    surveillance of **168**.8
embedded water **218**.35
embryo cloning *see* human reproductive cloning
embryo donation for research **178**.37
embryo freezing, effects on health **178**.22
embryo selection **178**.28-32
embryo splitting **211**.24
embryonic stem cells **211**.28, 29-30, 35-6
    stem cell research
        Catholic Church opposition **178**.35
        ethical issues **178**.33-5
        humanist view **178**.36-7
    see also therapeutic cloning
embryos
    hybrid **178**.35
    moral status **178**.33-4; **211**.31, 34
    and stem cell research **211**.31-2
EMDR (Eye Movement Desensitizing and Reprocessing)
    213.34
emergency contraception **173**.5, 25; **176**.27; **182**.5

emergency treatment
    drug abuse **228**.2
    drug overdose **199**.14
  self-harmers **199**.13-14
emissions
    reduction **200**.15
    standards **200**.15
    transport **200**.14, 22
    see also greenhouse gas emissions
Emissions Trading Scheme and airlines **222**.14-15
emotional abuse **179**.1; **224**.1, 3
    and children's mental health **201**.3
    signs of **179**.5
emotional distress and self-harm **199**.2
emotional extremes and self-harm **199**.10-11
emotional health
    and homelessness **189**.9
    see also mental health
emotional impact
    of divorce **166**.22-4
    of redundancy **183**.11
emotional signs of stress **206**.9, 19
employees
    gay and lesbian **225**.9
    surveillance **168**.9. 27, 38
employers
    involvement in schools **219**.26
    links with universities **209**.29
    views on qualifications **209**.3
    workforce monitoring by GPS **168**.27
    workplace monitoring **168**.38
employment
    and age discrimination **159**.8-13
    dementia sufferers **201**.11
    difficulty finding jobs **180**.34-5; **235**.6
    Disability Symbol **197**.26-7
    of disabled people **197**.20-21, 24-5, 26-7
    as economic indicator **180**.5
    employment status and smoking **188**.2
    ex-offenders **223**.26-7
    ex-service personnel **213**.32
    and free trade **226**.13-14
    and gender **221**.1-2, 18, 19, 27-9, 37
    and globalisation **226**.22
    graduates **185**.30, 31-2, 36-7
      value of extra-curricula interests **185**.7
    and homelessness **189**.33
    international labour standards **229**.14-16
    living wage for garment workers **229**.13
    and mental health sufferers **201**.11, 22-3, 27
    Millennium Development Goal **235**.26
    migrant workers *see* migrant workers
    and obesity **162**.21; **205**.20
    and online reputation **230**.32
    past retirement age **159**.10, 15
    and population growth **220**.6
    by private sector businesses **227**.4
    and race discrimination **172**.16-19
    and recession **180**.3
    from recycling **161**.2
    rights
      awareness of **183**.10
      disability rights **197**.20-21, 24-5, 26-7
      international standards **229**.14-16
      maternity rights **191**.37-8
      parental leave **191**.34 39
      paternity rights **191**.34-5, 39
      and religious belief **215**.23-4
    students **180**.29
    tourism industry **222**.21, 30
      Britain **222**.4
      youth training scheme **222**.31
    young people and the law **180**.20
    see also hours of work; jobs; part-time jobs; unemployment; women in the workforce; work-life balance; workplace bullying; workplace stress
Employment Assistance Programmes (EAPs) **206**.27
empty forest syndrome **193**.20
empty nest syndrome **191**.29
empty shops **207**.9
End Child Exploitation campaign **202**.2
End of Life Assistance (Scotland) Bill **217**.30

Vol. numbers appear first (in bold) followed by page numbers; a change in volume is preceded by a semi-**colon**.

Vol. 159   An Ageing Population
Vol. 161   Waste Issues
Vol. 162   Staying Fit
Vol. 164   The AIDS Crisis
Vol. 166   Marriage and Cohabitation
Vol. 168   Privacy and Surveillance
Vol. 172   Racial and Ethnic Discrimination
Vol. 173   Sexual Health
Vol. 174   Selling Sex
Vol. 175   Citizenship and Participation
Vol. 176   Health Issues for Young People
Vol. 177   Crime in the UK
Vol. 178   Reproductive Ethics
Vol. 179   Tackling Child Abuse
Vol. 180   Money and Finances
Vol. 181   The Housing Issue
Vol. 182   Teenage Conceptions
Vol. 183   Work and Employment
Vol. 184   Understanding Eating Disorders
Vol. 185   Student Matters
Vol. 186   Cannabis Use
Vol. 187   Health and the State
Vol. 188   Tobacco and Health

Vol. 189   The Homeless Population
Vol. 190   Coping with Depression
Vol. 191   The Changing Family
Vol. 192   Bereavement and Grief
Vol. 193   Endangered Species
Vol. 194   Responsible Drinking
Vol. 195   Alternative Medicine
Vol. 196   Censorship Issues
Vol. 197   Living with Disability
Vol. 198   Sport and Society
Vol. 199   Self-Harming and Suicide
Vol. 200   Sustainable Transport
Vol. 201   Mental Wellbeing
Vol. 202   Child Exploitation
Vol. 203   The Gambling Problem
Vol. 204   The Energy Crisis
Vol. 205   Nutrition and Diet
Vol. 206   Coping with Stress
Vol. 207   Consumerism and Ethics
Vol. 208   Genetic Modification
Vol. 209   Education and Society
Vol. 210   The Media
Vol. 211   Biotechnology and Cloning

Vol. 212   International Terrorism
Vol. 213   The Armed Forces
Vol. 214   Vegetarian Diets
Vol. 215   Religion in Society
Vol. 216   Tackling Climate Change
Vol. 217   Euthanasia and Assisted Suicide
Vol. 218   A Sustainable Future
Vol. 219   Class and Social Mobility
Vol. 220   Population Growth and Migration
Vol. 221   Equality and Gender Roles
Vol. 222   Tourism and Travel
Vol. 223   Crime. Punishment and Justice
Vol. 224   Domestic and Relationship Abuse
Vol. 225   LGBT Equality
Vol. 226   Globalisation and Trade
Vol. 227   Ethics in Business
Vol. 228   Illegal Drug Use
Vol. 229   Protecting Human Rights
Vol. 230   Evolution of the Internet
Vol. 231   The Abortion Debate
Vol. 232   Bullying in our Society
Vol. 233   Exploring Animal Rights
Vol. 234   Skin Deep - debating body image
Vol. 235   The Poverty Crisis

end-of-life rights information line **217**.37
End Violence Against Women (EVAW) Coalitition **224**.31
endangered species **193**.1-2
    butterflies **193**.36
    conservation work by zoos **233**.25, 26
    elephants **193**.19
    fish **193**.30
    invertebrates **193**.26
    pollinating insects **193**.27-8
    primates **193**.22-3
    tigers **193**.18
    in the UK **193**.31-2, 35, 36
    whales and dolphins **193**.29
    wildlife tourism **222**.26
    see also extinction; wildlife
endocrine disrupting chemicals **193**.16-17
endogenous (unipolar) depression **190**.10, 22-3
endometriosis **178**.4
energy **204**.1-39
    and consumer choice **218**.10
    energy companies, human rights considerations **229**.9
    energy policies
        EU **204**.30-31
        UK **204**.7-8, 28-9
    industry trends **204**.1
    microgeneration **204**.35
    renewable *see* renewable energy
    saving through recycling **161**.22
    storage **204**.37
    from waste **161**.20, 38, 39
    see also fuel poverty
energy consumption **204**.1
energy efficiency
    in the home **181**.39; **235**.16
    and sustainable housing **181**.39
    see also renewable energy
England
    abortion law **231**.3
    biodiversity loss **193**.31-2
    homelessness statistics **189**.3
    NHS provision **187**.29, 30
    rough sleepers **189**.16
    teenage pregnancy **182**.2, 7, 10
entrepreneurship
    aspirations **183**.7; **227**.6
    challenges to **227**.8
    developing countries **235**.33-5
    government initiative **227**.7
Entry to Employment (e2e) **183**.29
environment
    and agriculture **214**.16, 17,18-19, 21, 22, 23, 26
    definition **218**.1
    environmental causes of migration **220**.20, 38, 39
    and food production **205**.30, 31-2
        organic farming **205**.34, 35
    sustainable housing **181**.39
    and vegetarian food production **214**.26
    and vegetarianism **214**.15-27
    see also environmental impact; sustainable development;
wildlife

environmental governance, international **193**.12
environmental impact
    biodegradable products **218**.37
    biofuels **204**.33-4
    chemical pollutants **218**.38-9
    free trade **226**.32
    GM crops **208**.20-21, 22, 29
    globalisation **226**.4
    meat production **214**.18-19, 20-21; 23
    non-agricultural market access (NAMA) **226**.15-16
    population growth **218**.26-7, 28; **220**.4, 6-7, 14
    tourism **222**.21, 22, 25, 27, 28, 29
    transport **200**.1, 14-15, 16, 22, 24-5
        reducing **200**.15, 19-20, 25
environmental justice **218**.3-4
environmental retailing **207**.34
environmental sustainability *see* sustainability
environmental tobacco smoke *see* passive smoking
environmental tourism *see* ecotourism
epilepsy and exercise **198**.23
Equal Love campaign **225**.33
equal pay *see* gender pay gap
Equal Pay Act **221**.35-6
equality
    and faith schools **215**.18-19, 20
    legislation and religious belief **215**.25
Equality Act 2010 **183**.13; **221**.3, 36
    and LGBT people in schools **225**.6
    and mental health **201**.31
Equality Bill **172**.7, 19
Equality and Human Rights Commission **197**.25; **229**.34
equality at work **183**.12, 26-7
Essentials magazine, diversity award **234**.38
ethical consumerism **202**.13; **207**.23-39; **226**.38
    and child labour **202**.13-14
    statistics **207**.24
ethical food, labelling costs **207**.29
ethical investment and tax compliance **227**.33
ethical tourism *see* ecotourism; responsible travel; sustainable
tourism
ethical trade *see* fair trade
Ethical Trading Initiative (ETI) **226**.27
ethical volunteering **222**.38-9
ethics
    and abortion **231**.16-29
    and animal cloning **211**.10
    and biotechnology **211**.6
    of euthanasia and assisted suicide **217**.1-23
    of human cloning **211**.8-9, 26-7
    and stem cell research **211**.30-31, 34
    and tourism industry **222**.31-2
ethnic diversity, Britain **172**.30
ethnic equality, public opinion **229**.12
ethnic minorities
    and British identity **175**.9
    and feelings of discrimintation **175**.7
    and low income households **235**.7-8
    and mental health problems **201**.2
    representation in Parliament **175**.21
    women and poverty **221**.34
    see also Asian people; black people; employment and

racism; racism
ethnic origin
    and education **172**.14-16
    and identity **172**.26-39
    poverty and educational achievement **209**.13-14
    rough sleepers **189**.17
ethnic stereotypes
    reducing through tourism **222**.30
ethnocentric attitude **172**.24-5
Europe
    attitudes to biotechnology **211**.5-6
    child soldiers **202**.33
    domestic violence treaty **224**.32-3
    human rights treaties **168**.3
    IVF availability **178**.8
    and LGBT equality **225**.39
    press freedom **196**.2
    young people's feelings of European identity **175**.12
    see also European Union
European Commission on Human Rights **168**.3
European Committee of Social Rights, and corporal punishment **179**.31
European Convention on Human Rights **229**.1, 8, 36
    and privacy **168**.3
European Court of Human Rights
    death penalty cases **229**.39
    and DNA records **168**.12
    margin of appreciation **229**.6
    and privacy **168**.3
European Environment Agency (EEA) **200**.22
European Union
    animal welfare legislation **233**.2
    child abuse laws **179**.29
    complementary medicine research **195**.16
    and corporal punishment legislation **179**.31
    electricity markets **204**.11-12
    energy scenarios **204**.30-31
    entry-exit system **168**.9
    environmental policy **218**.7-8
    and GM crops **208**.11, 12
    human rights treaties **168**.3

immigration decline **220**.31
and LGBT equality **225**.11-13
migration to UK **220**.24-5
surveillance in **168**.9
trafficking laws **179**.29
transport policies **200**.15
views of young people **175**.12
wind energy **204**.11
euthanasia **217**.1-39
    arguments against **217**.2, 3-4, 5-6, 7-8
    arguments for **217**.3, 9-10, 11-12
    definitions **217**.1, 5
    doctors' opposition to **217**.22
    involuntary 5, 32
    and the law **217**.1, 24-39
    occurrence in UK **217**.24-5
    in other countries **217**.2
    public attitudes to **217**.23, 34
    see also advance directives; assisted suicide; physician assisted suicide (PAS)
evidence
    obtained under torture **229**.21-2
    secret intelligence to be allowed in court **223**.21-2
ex-offenders
    and employment **223**.26-7
    role in cutting youth crime **223**.18
ex-service personnel **213**.31-9
    finding employment **213**.32
    homelessness **189**.6; **213**.35
    mental health **213**.33-4
    as mentors to young people **213**.32
    in prison **213**.4, 36, 37-9
exams
    A-levels as predictor of degree performance **209**.12; **219**.32
    and pressure on schools **209**.4
    reform **209**.6
    standards **209**.7-10
    see also A-levels; GCSEs
exercise **162**.6; 29-34; **176**.6-7
    and the ageing process **159**.33; **162**.12

Vol. numbers appear first (in bold) followed by page numbers; a change in volume is preceded by a semi-**colon**.

Vol. 159 An Ageing Population
Vol. 161 Waste Issues
Vol. 162 Staying Fit
Vol. 164 The AIDS Crisis
Vol. 166 Marriage and Cohabitation
Vol. 168 Privacy and Surveillance
Vol. 172 Racial and Ethnic Discrimination
Vol. 173 Sexual Health
Vol. 174 Selling Sex
Vol. 175 Citizenship and Participation
Vol. 176 Health Issues for Young People
Vol. 177 Crime in the UK
Vol. 178 Reproductive Ethics
Vol. 179 Tackling Child Abuse
Vol. 180 Money and Finances
Vol. 181 The Housing Issue
Vol. 182 Teenage Conceptions
Vol. 183 Work and Employment
Vol. 184 Understanding Eating Disorders
Vol. 185 Student Matters
Vol. 186 Cannabis Use
Vol. 187 Health and the State
Vol. 188 Tobacco and Health

Vol. 189 The Homeless Population
Vol. 190 Coping with Depression
Vol. 191 The Changing Family
Vol. 192 Bereavement and Grief
Vol. 193 Endangered Species
Vol. 194 Responsible Drinking
Vol. 195 Alternative Medicine
Vol. 196 Censorship Issues
Vol. 197 Living with Disability
Vol. 198 Sport and Society
Vol. 199 Self-Harming and Suicide
Vol. 200 Sustainable Transport
Vol. 201 Mental Wellbeing
Vol. 202 Child Exploitation
Vol. 203 The Gambling Problem
Vol. 204 The Energy Crisis
Vol. 205 Nutrition and Diet
Vol. 206 Coping with Stress
Vol. 207 Consumerism and Ethics
Vol. 208 Genetic Modification
Vol. 209 Education and Society
Vol. 210 The Media
Vol. 211 Biotechnology and Cloning

Vol. 212 International Terrorism
Vol. 213 The Armed Forces
Vol. 214 Vegetarian Diets
Vol. 215 Religion in Society
Vol. 216 Tackling Climate Change
Vol. 217 Euthanasia and Assisted Suicide
Vol. 218 A Sustainable Future
Vol. 219 Class and Social Mobility
Vol. 220 Population Growth and Migration
Vol. 221 Equality and Gender Roles
Vol. 222 Tourism and Travel
Vol. 223 Crime. Punishment and Justice
Vol. 224 Domestic and Relationship Abuse
Vol. 225 LGBT Equality
Vol. 226 Globalisation and Trade
Vol. 227 Ethics in Business
Vol. 228 Illegal Drug Use
Vol. 229 Protecting Human Rights
Vol. 230 Evolution of the Internet
Vol. 231 The Abortion Debate
Vol. 232 Bullying in our Society
Vol. 233 Exploring Animal Rights
Vol. 234 Skin Deep - debating body image
Vol. 235 The Poverty Crisis

barriers to **162**.24, 29
and body image **176**.7
children **162**.6, 26, 28, 29; **176**.3
effect on weight **162**.28, 29
lack of exercise **162**.13, 15, 25
compulsive **162**.39; **184**.7
and depression **162**.37, 38; **190**.3, 7, 38
and eating disorders **184**.32
and fluid intake **205**.28
government strategy **162**.18
and health **162**.11-12, 29-31
and health problems **198**.23
lack of see inactivity
and life expectancy **159**.33
and mental health **162**.37, 38; **190**.3, 38
motivation for **162**.30-31
and obesity **162**.28, 29, 36
older people **159**.39
and pregnancy **182**.15
recommended amounts **162**.30
statistics **162**.6
and stress reduction **206**.33, 37
and vegetarian diet **214**.29
and weight loss **162**.20
when not to exercise **162**.31-2
in the workplace **162**.23, 24
and young people **176**.6-7
exhaust gases see emissions, transport
exotic species
in the wild, Britain **193**.39
trade in **193**.20-21
Expand SkillForce Core Programme **213**.32
Expect Respect campaign (domestic violence) **179**.19
expression, freedom of see freedom of expression
Extended Determinate Sentence **223**.21
extended licence period **223**.21
extreme pornography and the law **174**.20, 21, 22-5
extremism
in schools **212**.12
at universities **212**.13-14

F

Facebook
addiction to **230**.15
censorship of sexual content **196**.37
and privacy **168**.35; **210**.33-4
reporting inappropriate content **232**.35
factory farming **233**.3, 7-8
fairness, children's rights to **229**.26
fairness complaints against broadcasters **196**.20
Fairtrade **207**.32, 33; **226**.30, 31, 36-7
ineffectiveness **207**.33
faith-based medicine, difficulty of regulating **195**.36
faith communities, role in society **172**.39
faith healing **195**.5
faith schools **209**.22-3, 24; **215**.17-20
and free schools programme **215**.21-2
and sex education **173**.34-5

fallopian tube damage and infertility **178**.4
falls, older people **159**.4, 6
false memory syndrome **179**.26-9
families
abuse of older people **159**.17
of cannabis users **186**.23-5
changing family patterns **166**.15; **191**.1-4
of disabled young people **197**.18-19
of drug users **186**.23-5
family breakdown
and children's wellbeing **191**.9
and paternal contact **191**.11
and youth homelessness **189**.21, 26, 27
see also divorce
family structure, effect on children's character **191**.6
and gambling **203**.33
and homelessness **189**.29-32
income, and educational attainment **219**.22, 23, 25-6, 27-8, 29-30, 34
and the Mental Health Act **190**.11
of sexually exploited children **202**.23
spending power falling **207**.8
support during divorce **166**.29, 30, 31
support for pregnant teenagers **182**.16
support to prevent child crime **223**.32
see also lone parents; parents; stepfamilies
family planning
Millennium Development Goals **218**.39
and population control **218**.26-7
see also birth control; contraception
family planning clinics, use by teenagers **173**.9; **182**.1-2
farming see agriculture; organic farming
fashion industry
and body image **184**.24; **234**.5-6, 11
and fur trade **233**.19
and living wage **229**.13
fats in diet **205**.1, 3, 24
food labelling **205**.11
need to reduce fat content of food **205**.18
fatalities see deaths
fathers
and childcare **221**.5
contact with children after family break-up **191**.11
parenting roles **191**.30-33
paternity leave **183**.18, 22, 24; **191**.34-5, 39; **221**.4-5
post-natal depression **190**.16-17
teenage fathers **182**.17
work-family balance **183**.22-3; **191**.34-5
fatty acids
omega 3 **214**.29, 33
in red meat **214**.35
feelings after bereavement **192**.1-2, 3, 9-10, 11, 13, 15, 20
fees, university **185**.11, 17, 29, 36
female condoms (femidom) **173**.24
female genital mutilation **224**.3-4, 37
femininity and dieting **234**.8
feminism
and pornography **174**.23
as reason for not marrying **166**.10
fertility

effect of abortion **231**.7
effect of cannabis use **186**.16
problems **178**.2-5
worldwide **220**.2, 4, 9, 13, 15
fertility tourism **178**.18, 20
fetuses
  age of viability **231**.22
  fetal rights **231**.17, 18
  fetal stem cells used to treat stroke victims **211**.33
fighting animals **233**.6, 17, 27
films
  classification **196**.13-16
  influence on young people smoking **188**.25
  public opinion **196**.15-16
filtered cigarettes **188**.10
finance and football **198**.11-12
finance, students *see* students and money matters
financial abuse **224**.1, 3
  and older people **159**.16
financial benefits *see* state benefits
financial companies, informing of a death **192**.32
financial crisis, global **180**.1-2
financial education **180**.36-9
financial expectations, young people **180**.20-21
financial freedom, older people **159**.20
financial implications of partner's death **192**.33
financial incentives
  for health care **187**.37
  for marriage **166**.5; **191**.2
  for reducing waste **161**.38
  for weight loss **162**.22-3
financial planning for old age **159**.21-2; **180**.8
  see also pensions
financial responsibility for children **166**.14-15, 34-5
financial sector taxes **235**.13-15
financial support to adult children
  by parents **191**.27-8
fingerprinting in schools **168**.30
Finland, regulation of pornography **174**.13
firearms offences **223**.5
fires caused by smoking **188**.22

first aid treatment for drug abuse effects **199**.14; **228**.2
first-past-the-post electoral system **175**.24-5
first-time buyers
  parental support **181**.1
  pessimism about owning homes **181**.5
fish, in diet **205**.3
  labelling rules **205**.12
  vegetarian diet **214**.1
fishing industry
  environmental impact **214**.17, 25-6
  and sustainability **193**.30; **218**.23
    buying sustainable fish **205**.32
fit notes **183**.8
fitness
  effects on ageing **159**.33, 34; **162**.12
  equipment for older people **159**.39
  government strategy **162**.17-18
  inequalities **162**.35
  and mental health **162**.37, 38
  motivation **162**.30-31
  myths **162**.33-4
  see also exercise
fitness industry, lack of effect on obesity **162**.35
five-a-day fruit and vegetable consumption **205**.1, 2, 17
flags **175**.2
flexible working **183**.16-27
  effect of recession **183**.1
  fathers **183**.22; **191**.34, 39
  and gender equality **221**.24
  mothers **191**.36
  options **183**.17, 18
  statistics **183**.20
flexitarian diet **214**.1
flood management **218**.6, 23
flour, labelling rules **205**.11-12
fluid intake **205**.27-8
fly-tipping **161**.16
foetus *see* fetuses
foil
  aluminium, recycling **161**.27
  provision to heroin users **228**.26

Vol. numbers appear first (in bold) followed by page numbers; a change in volume is preceded by a semi-**colon**.

Vol. 159 An Ageing Population
Vol. 161 Waste Issues
Vol. 162 Staying Fit
Vol. 164 The AIDS Crisis
Vol. 166 Marriage and Cohabitation
Vol. 168 Privacy and Surveillance
Vol. 172 Racial and Ethnic Discrimination
Vol. 173 Sexual Health
Vol. 174 Selling Sex
Vol. 175 Citizenship and Participation
Vol. 176 Health Issues for Young People
Vol. 177 Crime in the UK
Vol. 178 Reproductive Ethics
Vol. 179 Tackling Child Abuse
Vol. 180 Money and Finances
Vol. 181 The Housing Issue
Vol. 182 Teenage Conceptions
Vol. 183 Work and Employment
Vol. 184 Understanding Eating Disorders
Vol. 185 Student Matters
Vol. 186 Cannabis Use
Vol. 187 Health and the State
Vol. 188 Tobacco and Health

Vol. 189 The Homeless Population
Vol. 190 Coping with Depression
Vol. 191 The Changing Family
Vol. 192 Bereavement and Grief
Vol. 193 Endangered Species
Vol. 194 Responsible Drinking
Vol. 195 Alternative Medicine
Vol. 196 Censorship Issues
Vol. 197 Living with Disability
Vol. 198 Sport and Society
Vol. 199 Self-Harming and Suicide
Vol. 200 Sustainable Transport
Vol. 201 Mental Wellbeing
Vol. 202 Child Exploitation
Vol. 203 The Gambling Problem
Vol. 204 The Energy Crisis
Vol. 205 Nutrition and Diet
Vol. 206 Coping with Stress
Vol. 207 Consumerism and Ethics
Vol. 208 Genetic Modification
Vol. 209 Education and Society
Vol. 210 The Media
Vol. 211 Biotechnology and Cloning

Vol. 212 International Terrorism
Vol. 213 The Armed Forces
Vol. 214 Vegetarian Diets
Vol. 215 Religion in Society
Vol. 216 Tackling Climate Change
Vol. 217 Euthanasia and Assisted Suicide
Vol. 218 A Sustainable Future
Vol. 219 Class and Social Mobility
Vol. 220 Population Growth and Migration
Vol. 221 Equality and Gender Roles
Vol. 222 Tourism and Travel
Vol. 223 Crime, Punishment and Justice
Vol. 224 Domestic and Relationship Abuse
Vol. 225 LGBT Equality
Vol. 226 Globalisation and Trade
Vol. 227 Ethics in Business
Vol. 228 Illegal Drug Use
Vol. 229 Protecting Human Rights
Vol. 230 Evolution of the Internet
Vol. 231 The Abortion Debate
Vol. 232 Bullying in our Society
Vol. 233 Exploring Animal Rights
Vol. 234 Skin Deep - debating body image
Vol. 235 The Poverty Crisis

food
in the Army **213**.1
from cloned animals **211**.10-19
public attitudes **211**.6
safety **211**.18, 19
global food system **218**.29-30
GM food *see* genetically modified (GM) food
hunger *see* hunger
in-vitro meat **211**.20-21
labelling costs **207**.29
and mental health **190**.3
organic **205**.30, 33, 34-6
supplies
and climate change **216**.6-7, 10
and factory farming **233**.8
and GM crops **208**.19, 23-4, 32, 34-6
and meat production **214**.5, 16
and population growth **220**.3-4, 6
and young people **176**.8-9
see also diet; eating disorders; fat intake; healthy eating;
meat consumption; vegetarian food
food additives **205**.14-16
organic food **205**.34
food advertising and children **205**.38
food industry
and climate change **205**.30
and the economy **205**.29-30
need to reduce salt and fat in food **205**.18
food labelling
ethical labelling costs **207**.29
GM food **208**.8
misleading claims **205**.39
nutritional information **205**.13
organic food **205**.33
regulations **205**.11-12
salt content **205**.26
food and nutrition **205**.1-28
balanced diet **205**.2-3, 4-5
teenagers **176**.8-9
see also diet; healthy eating; nutrition; vegetarianism
food packaging
recycling tins **161**.27
food poisoning **205**.5
food poverty in UK **235**.17
food production, environmental impact **205**.30; **214**.16,
17, 18-19, 20-21
food safety **205**.5
genetically modified food **208**.2, 24
and organic farming **205**.34, 36
food security
and GM crops **208**.19,23-4, 34-6
food standards and labelling **205**.11-12
Food Standards Agency (FSA) and GM food **208**.7
food waste **161**.4, 10-11, 19; **205**.31, 32
football
Asian players **198**.24
finance **198**.11-12
and homophobia **198**.25, 26
and racism **172**.2
and violence **198**.13
WAGS (wives and girlfriends) **198**.15-17

footwear for exercise **162**.32
forced labour **229**.15; **227**.29-3-0
and human trafficking **229**.17
forced marriages **166**.17-20; **224**.3, 14-15, 36-7
action against **220**.30
and Islam **215**.12
forced migration **220**.36-7
forced retirement **183**.14-15
Ford factory equal pay strike **221**.35, 36
foreign holidays, attitudes to **222**.2
foreign nationals
deportation and the Human Rights Act **229**.4-5
prisoners **223**.25
foreign travel, young people **175**.12
forests
and climate change **216**.11, 14-15
dryland forests **218**.21
empty forest syndrome **193**.20
protection **193**.4
rainforest destruction **193**.1, 5
rainforest protection, UN programme **218**.20-21
restoration **193**.15
see also deforestation
40 Days for Life campaign **231**.34, 35
fossil fuels **204**.6, 25
energy industry statistics **204**.1
subsidies **204**.4
see also oil
fostering
as alternative to abortion **231**.8
foster parents' refusal to promote homosexual lifestyle
225.34
foundation stage education
and character skills **219**.34-5
and social mobility **219**.17-18
Frank anti-drug helpline **186**.26-7
fraud
costs of **207**.21-2
free schools **209**.19-21
and faith schools **215**.21-2
free speech **196**.1-12
and the Internet **230**.37, 38-9
free trade **172**.12-13; **226**.13-14, 29-30, 33
and employment **226**.13-14
negative effects **226**.13-14, 32
and poverty **226**.14, 29-30, 33
see also trade liberalisation
freedom of expression **196**.37
global public opinion **229**.11-12
and the Internet **230**.37, 38-9
versus privacy **229**.5
freedom of information **196**.38
and the Internet **230**.37, 38-9
Freedom of Information Act **168**.10-11
freedom of information complaints **168**.4
freedom of the press, global study **196**.1-2
freedom from surveillance **196**.38
freezing
eggs **178**.23
embryos **178**.22
freight transport trends **200**.22

freshwater resources **193**.5
    impact of climate change **216**.6, 10
Friends of the Earth
    opposition to non-agricultural market access **226**.15
    16
    views on free trade **226**.15
fringe medicine *see* complementary medicine (CM)
front-temporal lobar degeneration (FTLD) **201**.10
frontbenchers **175**.17
fruit and vegetable consumption **162**.6; **205**.1, 2, 17
fruit juices **205**.28
    labelling rules **205**.12
FSA (Food Standards Agency) and GM food **208**.7
FTSE 100 companies, use of tax havens **227**.35-6
fuel cells **204**.27, 38
fuel efficient homes **235**.16
fuel poverty **204**.23; **218**.3; **235**.15-16
    and microgeneration **204**.36
    pensioners **159**.3
full-time parents, stress **191**.35
fundamentalism, Islamic **212**.32
funding
    EMA **209**.17, 18
    faith schools **215**.17
    further education **209**.17
    higher education **185**.17, 35-6; **209**.29, 31-2, 35
        see also tuition fees
    HIV prevention programmes **164**.23, 39
    homeopathy on the NHS **195**.16, 17-22, 24-5
    NHS **187**.1, 3, 11-12, 30
    road network **200**.6, 7, 9-10
    sport
        disability sports **198**.18, 20, 21
        funding cuts **198**.6-7
funerals **192**.30-31, 34-7
fur trade **233**.3-4, 18-19
further education, funding **209**.17
    benefits of **183**.33, 34

G8 summit, climate change agreement **216**.37
Galileo satellite system **168**.27
gambling **203**.1-39
    addiction *see* problem gambling
    definition **203**.5
    effects **203**.21-2, 28-9
    forms of **203**.4
    giving up **203**.6-7
    history of **203**.5
    online gambling **203**.28-9
        participation rates **203**.4
        women **203**.35-6
        young people **203**.17
    participation in **203**.3-4
        young people **203**.12, 16-17
    problem gamblers *see* problem gambling
    reasons for **203**.1, 9, 21, 32-3
    social context **203**.32-3
    women **203**.26, 35-6
    young people **203**.9-18
        Internet gambling **203**.16-18
        problem gambling **203**.12, 15, 16, 20
        reasons for gambling **203**.9
    see also casinos; National Lottery; problem gambling
gamete donation *see* egg donation; sperm donation
gamete intrafallopian transfer (GIFT) **178**.11
gamete market **178**.12
gaming
    and bullying **232**.25
    women **230**.2
gaming machines **203**.4
gamma-butyrolactone (GBL) **194**.9
gamma-hydroxybutyrate (GHB) **194**.9
gamophobia (fear of marriage) **166**.9
gang injunctions (gangbos) **223**.35-6
gangs **189**.28
    and crime **223**.6-7, 13-15, 35-6
gap years **185**.31; **183**.20

popular destinations **222**.19
garden-grabbing, political party policies **181**.23
garment industry, campaign for living wage **229**.13
gas
  green **204**.24
  natural gas industry trends **204**.1
gasification **204**.6
gastric surgery for weight loss **162**.3
gay couples *see* same-sex relationships
gay men
  and adoption **191**.22-5
  awareness of gay feelings **225**.1
  and blood donation **225**.36-7
  and HIV **164**.22
    HIV prevention campaigns **164**.24
    infection rate **164**.16, 17, 22
    life expectancy **164**.9
  young people, mental health problems **201**.3
  see also homosexuality
GCSEs
  as predictor of degree results **219**.32
  reform **209**.6
GDP (Gross Domestic Product) as poor measure of living
standards **226**.14
geep (sheep-goat chimera) 10
gender **221**.1, 11
  and alcohol consumption, young people **194**.2
  and alcohol-related deaths **194**.13
  and Alzheimer's disease **159**.36
  and attitudes to higher education **209**.27
  and attitudes to school **209**.11
  and attitudes to sex **173**.12-13
  and colour preferences **221**.7-8
  and compulsive shopping **207**.6
  and education *see* gender and education
  and employment **221**.1-2, 18, 19, 27-9, 37
    see also women in the workforce
  and gambling **203**.16
  and graduate unemployment **185**.32
  and household financial roles **180**.18-19
  and household tasks **221**.6
  and Internet usage **230**.2-4
  and media usage **210**.12
  and mental health problems **190**.18-19
  and the news **210**.6-8
  and parental roles **191**.30-32
  and pay *see* gender pay gap
  and smoking **188**.1
  and suicide **199**.24, 28, 32
  and work **221**.27-9
  see also gender pay gap; men; women
gender abortions **231**.18, 30-31
gender assignation **225**.8
gender-based violence *see* domestic abuse; rape
gender dysphoria **225**.20, 21-2
gender and education
  attitudes to school **209**.11
  higher education **185**.14; **209**.27
gender equality
  international initiatives **221**.2
  and Islam **215**.12

legal rights **221**.2, 3
  Olympic Games **198**.19
Gender Equality Duty (GED) **225**.7
gender identity clinics **225**.20
  Tavistock and Portman service **225**.21, 22, 23
gender identity disorder **225**.20
gender inequality **221**.1-2, 33-5, 37
  at work **221**.1-2, 18, 19, 27, 37
  definition **221**.11
  and HIV **164**.5-6
  worldwide **221**.1-2, 33-9
gender pay audits **221**.24
gender pay gap **221**.22-5, 27-8, 35-6, 37
Gender Recognition Act 2004 **225**.6, 20, 27
gender quotas, company boards **221**.16, 21
gender stereotyping **221**.11, 33
  and employment **221**.23, 28, 29
  and toys **221**.7-8
gender variant **225**.20
gene doping **198**.30
gene mapping **208**.13
general elections **175**.22
generalised anxiety disorder (GAD) **206**.11, 14-15
genes **178**.3
  and ageing **159**.2, 32
  and Alzheimer's disease **159**.36
  and anxiety **206**.3
  and depression **190**.2, 4, 12-13
    bipolar disorder **190**.11, 12-13
    teenage depression **190**.25
  and gambling addiction **203**.30-31
  human genes implanted into animals **233**.39
  and mental health **201**.33
  and obesity **162**.9-10
  and sexual orientation **225**.1-2
  and stress **206**.30-31
genetic modification
  applications **208**.6, 19-22, 37-8
  arguments against **208**.3-4, 5, 17
  arguments for **208**.2, 3, 17
  definition **208**.1, 3
  and the environment **208**.20, 22, 29
  generations of plants **208**.1-2
  human cells transplanted into animals **233**.39
  method **208**.14
  risks **208**.17
  testing **208**.1
  see also genetically modified animals; genetically modified
crops; genetically modified food
genetic resources, international cooperation **193**.12
genetically modified (GM) animals **208**.3, 13-14, 37-9
  chickens **208**.14, 37-8
  experiments on **208**.37-8
  fish **214**.25-6
  salmon **208**.31, 39
genetically modified (GM) crops **208**.1-2
  and animal feed **208**.8, 24
  arguments for and against **208**.5, 9-10, 17, 34
  crop area **208**.9, 10
  cross-contamination **208**.24, 26
  developing countries **208**.10

and food supply **208**.19, 23-4, 32, 34-6
   risks **208**.27-8
   UK **208**.5, 17-18
genetically modified (GM) food **208**.5-8
   arguments against **208**.23-4, 31-2
   effects on health **208**.5, 8, 19-20
   public attitudes to **208**.18, 29-30; **211**.6
   safety **208**.1, 2, 7
genital herpes **173**.18, 21
genital warts **173**.18, 20-21
Genuine Occupational Requirement and sexual orientation **225**.28
Geographic Information Systems (GIS) **168**.27
geothermal energy **204**.3, 27
Germany, regulation of prostitution **174**.13
gestational surrogacy **178**.7, 13
Getting it Right campaign **197**.39
Ghana
   impact of free trade **226**.29, 32
   income growth **235**.30
   withdrawal of aid due to anti-gay laws **225**.14
ghettos, myths about **172**.33
ghost tourism **222**.16
Gibson inquiry into use of torture **229**.22, 23
ginger bullying **232**.16
girls' schools **221**.31-2
girls and young women
   aspiring to be WAGS **198**.15-17
   attitudes to politics **175**.33-4
   attitudes to school **209**.11
   attitudes to sex **173**.12-13
   and body image **184**.17-18, 27; **234**.9, 25-6, 31
   and child labour **202**.5
   child soldiers **202**.32, 35-6
   and cosmetic surgery **234**.33, 34
   and cricket **198**.4
   dieting **184**.22
   and education **221**.31-2, 35, 38-9
     effect on population control **220**.7
     programmes in developing countries **229**.27-8
   effects of mother's dieting **184**.21-2

and prostitution **174**.11-12
   sexualisation of **174**.27, 30, 38-9; **221**.9-10
   single-sex education **221**.31-2
   toy preferences **221**.7-8
   violence against **224**.28-31
GIS (Geographic Information Systems) **168**.27
'Give Yourself a Chance' campaign **234**.34
glamour modelling as career aspiration **174**.30
glamping **222**.20
glass **161**.5, 22
   recycling **161**.24, 27
glass ceiling **221**.21-2
Global AIDS Alliance **164**.8, 28
global financial crisis **180**.1-2; **235**.13-14
Global Media Monitoring Project **210**.6-8
Global Partnership on Forest Restoration (GPFLR) **193**.15
global positioning system (GPS)
   and surveillance **168**.27
global poverty **235**.23-39
   statistics **235**.23, 24
global trade **226**.26-39
global warming **216**.8, 9; **218**.19
   measurement **216**.26-7
   see also climate change; energy efficiency; greenhouse gas
     emissions
globalisation **226**.1-25
   definition **226**.1, 13
   effects of **226**.2, 13, 20-21, 24-5
   and ethical consumerism **207**.23
   need for international cooperation **226**.17-19, 21, 22-5
   and trade **226**.26-39
GM crops *see* genetically modified (GM) crops
golden rice **208**.19, 29, 35
gonorrhoea **173**.18, 21
'good' deaths **192**.8, 24
Google
   Google Earth **168**.26-7
   government censorship requests **196**.29
   Street View **210**.33
   withdrawal from China **196**.27-8, 29, 30
Government, UK **175**.17, 20

Vol. numbers appear first (in bold) followed by page numbers; a change in volume is preceded by a semi-**colon**.

Vol. 159 An Ageing Population	**Vol. 189** The Homeless Population	**Vol. 212** International Terrorism
Vol. 161 Waste Issues	**Vol. 190** Coping with Depression	**Vol. 213** The Armed Forces
Vol. 162 Staying Fit	**Vol. 191** The Changing Family	**Vol. 214** Vegetarian Diets
Vol. 164 The AIDS Crisis	**Vol. 192** Bereavement and Grief	**Vol. 215** Religion in Society
Vol. 166 Marriage and Cohabitation	**Vol. 193** Endangered Species	**Vol. 216** Tackling Climate Change
Vol. 168 Privacy and Surveillance	**Vol. 194** Responsible Drinking	**Vol. 217** Euthanasia and Assisted Suicide
Vol. 172 Racial and Ethnic Discrimination	**Vol. 195** Alternative Medicine	**Vol. 218** A Sustainable Future
Vol. 173 Sexual Health	**Vol. 196** Censorship Issues	**Vol. 219** Class and Social Mobility
Vol. 174 Selling Sex	**Vol. 197** Living with Disability	**Vol. 220** Population Growth and Migration
Vol. 175 Citizenship and Participation	**Vol. 198** Sport and Society	**Vol. 221** Equality and Gender Roles
Vol. 176 Health Issues for Young People	**Vol. 199** Self-Harming and Suicide	**Vol. 222** Tourism and Travel
Vol. 177 Crime in the UK	**Vol. 200** Sustainable Transport	**Vol. 223** Crime, Punishment and Justice
Vol. 178 Reproductive Ethics	**Vol. 201** Mental Wellbeing	**Vol. 224** Domestic and Relationship Abuse
Vol. 179 Tackling Child Abuse	**Vol. 202** Child Exploitation	**Vol. 225** LGBT Equality
Vol. 180 Money and Finances	**Vol. 203** The Gambling Problem	**Vol. 226** Globalisation and Trade
Vol. 181 The Housing Issue	**Vol. 204** The Energy Crisis	**Vol. 227** Ethics in Business
Vol. 182 Teenage Conceptions	**Vol. 205** Nutrition and Diet	**Vol. 228** Illegal Drug Use
Vol. 183 Work and Employment	**Vol. 206** Coping with Stress	**Vol. 229** Protecting Human Rights
Vol. 184 Understanding Eating Disorders	**Vol. 207** Consumerism and Ethics	**Vol. 230** Evolution of the Internet
Vol. 185 Student Matters	**Vol. 208** Genetic Modification	**Vol. 231** The Abortion Debate
Vol. 186 Cannabis Use	**Vol. 209** Education and Society	**Vol. 232** Bullying in our Society
Vol. 187 Health and the State	**Vol. 210** The Media	**Vol. 233** Exploring Animal Rights
Vol. 188 Tobacco and Health	**Vol. 211** Biotechnology and Cloning	**Vol. 234** Skin Deep - debating body image
		Vol. 235 The Poverty Crisis

body confidence campaign **234**.20-21, 37, 39
the Budget **180**.24
control of broadcasters **196**.18-19
domestic violence definitions **224**.34-7
finance, and smoking **188**.22, 23
funding for disabled children **197**.36
funding for higher education **180**.28, 33
Government departments **175**.20
healthy behaviour promotion **234**.11-12
and religion **215**.6
surveillance **168**.4-5, 7-8, 13-14, 27, 35
women's representation **221**.13, 15, 20, 37
see also Parliament
Government policies
on alcohol **194**.33
child poverty strategy **235**.19
on crime **223**.23-5
gang crime **223**.13-15
on drugs **186**.4, 35-6; **228**.24-7
see also classification of drugs
on education **209**.17, 18, 19, 24
academies **209**.25, 26
on genetically modified crops **208**.5
on health **162**.4-5, 9-10, 17-18, 22-3
on higher education **185**.25
on homelessness **189**.8, 34
and homeopathy **195**.23, 24, 25, 26-7
on housing **181**.23
missing affordable housing target **181**.6
houses of multiple occupation **181**.19-20
and integrated healthcare **195**.23
on mental health **201**.5
on plastic bags **161**.14
and obesity **205**.20-21
on preventing violence against women and girls **224**.28-31
on public health **219**.13
race equality **172**.20-21
in employment **172**.19
renewable energy **204**.4, 7-8, 15-16
sensible drinking guidelines *see* daily benchmarks on alcohol consumption
on sexually transmitted infections **173**.21
on smacking **179**.33
on smoking **188**.33-5
on social mobility **219**.17-21
waste strategy **161**.20
welfare reforms **235**.9, 10
Government targets on homelessness **189**.8
governments
control of the Internet **196**.32-5
Internet censorship requests **196**.29
GPs (general practitioners)
asking about patient's alcohol consumption **194**.33, 37-8
diagnosing depression **190**.31
and eating disorders **184**.36
patient survey **187**.16-17
registering at university **176**.5
relationship with patients **187**.31
surgery waiting times **187**.16
see also doctors
GPS *see* global positioning system
graduates
destinations **185**.31-2
earnings **183**.34; **185**.21, 32-4
employment **185**.31-2, 36-7
effect of recession **183**.1-2, 35-6
options after graduating **185**.30-31
starting salaries **183**.36
unemployment **180**.35
grandparents **191**.14-17
and childcare **191**.15, 16-17
grants, student **180**.28, 33; **185**.2
Great Seal of the Realm **175**.2
green belt land **181**.21, 36
green cars *see* fuel efficient cars
green gas **204**.24
green infrastructure **181**.36
green tourism *see* ecotourism; responsible travel; sustainable tourism
green waste **161**.28-9, 30
greenfield development **181**.22, 36
greenhouse effect **216**.1
greenhouse gases
emission reduction targets **216**.7, 33
emission trends **216**.7
emissions
from food production **205**.30
from livestock farming **214**.17, 18, 19, 21
from transport **200**.14, 15, 22
and GM crops **208**.22
see also carbon dioxide emissions
Greenland ice sheet **216**.15
greenwashing **222**.24
grief **192**.1-2, 3-4
before death **192**.6
public **192**.7-8
and young people **192**.9-23
grocery shopping, online **207**.10
grooming **174**.11-12; **202**.21, 25
online **179**.16; **230**.23-4
Gross Domestic Product (GDP) as poor measure of living standards **226**.14
growth hormones and sports drug abuse **198**.30
Guantánamo Bay **212**.33-5
torture of detainees **212**.36-7
guided busways **200**.30, 32
Guiding Principles on Business and Human Rights (UN) **227**.27, 28
guilt
children's feelings after bereavement **192**.13
and post traumatic stress disorder **201**.21
gun crime **223**.5
Gypsies **172**.23

H

habitat loss **193**.1
see also deforestation

haemophiliacs and HIV **164**.25
Haiti, debt and disater **226**.6
Halal slaughter **233**.16
halls of residence **209**.30
hallucinogens (psychedelics) **228**.3-4, 14
handbag dogs **233**.4
hangovers **194**.7
    and exercise **162**.32
happiness
    of children, effect of paretnal relationship **166**.32
    in marriage **166**.7-8
harassment
    definition **221**.3; **225**.28
    by journalists, Editor' Code **210**.28
    racial **172**.5, 17
    on grounds of sexual orientation **225**.28
hardening hypothesis (stopping smoking) **188**.17
hashish (cannabis resins) **186**.2, 7, 9
hate crime **172**.9
    anti-Muslim **215**.28-30
    homophobic **225**.29, 30-31, 32
hazardous waste **161**.6, 32; **218**.12
health **176**.1-39
    and alcohol
        benefits **194**.18
        risks **194**.6, 7, 15, 17, 18, 19, 22-3
    and anxiety **206**.10
    and body image **234**.10, 11
    and cannabis **186**.15-17, 28-9
    and car travel **200**.1, 23
    children's rights **229**.24
    and climate change **216**.7, 10
    and compulsive exercise **162**.39
    and drug abuse **228**.12-13
    exercising with health problems **198**.23
    and fuel poverty **235**.15-16
    and GM crops **208**.19-20, 29
    government strategies **162**.4-5, 9-10, 17-18, 22-3
    and homelessness **189**.12-13
    inequalities **235**.6-7
    and marital status **166**.15

    and meat consumption **214**.16, 34-5
    and obesity **162**.1-2, 5, 6, 7, 19, 25
    older people **159**.4, 6, 8, 34
    and organic produce **205**.34, 36
    and population growth **220**.2
    in pregnancy **182**.15
        employment rights **191**.37
    and salt intake **205**.25-6
    and smoking **188**.5-12, 15, 18, 19, 22
        benefits of giving up **188**.6, 9
        passive smoking **188**.5, 10-11, 12
        in pregnancy **188**.11, 31
    and social class **219**.11-13
    students **176**.5-6
    teenage parents and their children **182**.27
    tobacco pickers **188**.39
    travel health advice **222**.10
    UK health profile **187**.4, 11
    and vegetarian diets **205**.37; **214**.4-5, 9, 12, 28-33, 36-9
    see also mental health; mental illness; sexual health
health care
    discrimination, disabled people **197**.30, 38-9
    eating disorders treatment **184**.12, 33-9
    health checks as legal right **187**.32-3
    NHS **187**.1-23
        future proposals **187**.32-9
        problems **187**.25-31
    older people **159**.6
health education on smoking **176**.13
Health and Safety at Work Act and stress **206**.25, 28
health warnings on cigarette packs **188**.29
healthy eating **184**.32; **205**.2-3, 4-5, 17-18, 23
    children **162**.25-6; **176**.3
    and the environment **205**.31
    government strategies **162**.10, 17-18
    and meat consumption **214**.34-5
    obsession with healthy eating **184**.9
    and schools **205**.6-7
    and social class **162**.13-14
    and stress **206**.33

Vol. numbers appear first (in bold) followed by page numbers; a change in volume is preceded by a semi-**colon**.

Vol. 159	An Ageing Population	**Vol. 189**	The Homeless Population	**Vol. 212**	International Terrorism
Vol. 161	Waste Issues	**Vol. 190**	Coping with Depression	**Vol. 213**	The Armed Forces
Vol. 162	Staying Fit	**Vol. 191**	The Changing Family	**Vol. 214**	Vegetarian Diets
Vol. 164	The AIDS Crisis	**Vol. 192**	Bereavement and Grief	**Vol. 215**	Religion in Society
Vol. 166	Marriage and Cohabitation	**Vol. 193**	Endangered Species	**Vol. 216**	Tackling Climate Change
Vol. 168	Privacy and Surveillance	**Vol. 194**	Responsible Drinking	**Vol. 217**	Euthanasia and Assisted Suicide
Vol. 172	Racial and Ethnic Discrimination	**Vol. 195**	Alternative Medicine	**Vol. 218**	A Sustainable Future
Vol. 173	Sexual Health	**Vol. 196**	Censorship Issues	**Vol. 219**	Class and Social Mobility
Vol. 174	Selling Sex	**Vol. 197**	Living with Disability	**Vol. 220**	Population Growth and Migration
Vol. 175	Citizenship and Participation	**Vol. 198**	Sport and Society	**Vol. 221**	Equality and Gender Roles
Vol. 176	Health Issues for Young People	**Vol. 199**	Self-Harming and Suicide	**Vol. 222**	Tourism and Travel
Vol. 177	Crime in the UK	**Vol. 200**	Sustainable Transport	**Vol. 223**	Crime. Punishment and Justice
Vol. 178	Reproductive Ethics	**Vol. 201**	Mental Wellbeing	**Vol. 224**	Domestic and Relationship Abuse
Vol. 179	Tackling Child Abuse	**Vol. 202**	Child Exploitation	**Vol. 225**	LGBT Equality
Vol. 180	Money and Finances	**Vol. 203**	The Gambling Problem	**Vol. 226**	Globalisation and Trade
Vol. 181	The Housing Issue	**Vol. 204**	The Energy Crisis	**Vol. 227**	Ethics in Business
Vol. 182	Teenage Conceptions	**Vol. 205**	Nutrition and Diet	**Vol. 228**	Illegal Drug Use
Vol. 183	Work and Employment	**Vol. 206**	Coping with Stress	**Vol. 229**	Protecting Human Rights
Vol. 184	Understanding Eating Disorders	**Vol. 207**	Consumerism and Ethics	**Vol. 230**	Evolution of the Internet
Vol. 185	Student Matters	**Vol. 208**	Genetic Modification	**Vol. 231**	The Abortion Debate
Vol. 186	Cannabis Use	**Vol. 209**	Education and Society	**Vol. 232**	Bullying in our Society
Vol. 187	Health and the State	**Vol. 210**	The Media	**Vol. 233**	Exploring Animal Rights
Vol. 188	Tobacco and Health	**Vol. 211**	Biotechnology and Cloning	**Vol. 234**	Skin Deep - debating body image
				Vol. 235	The Poverty Crisis

tyranny **162**.16
and vegetarian diets **205**.37-8; **214**.28-30, 33, 36, 37, 38-9
young people **176**.3, 8-9
see also diet; food and nutrition
Health Protection Agency (HPA) **187**.6
healthy weight maintenance *see* weight management
heart
effects of alcohol **194**.18
effects of salt intake **205**.25
effects of smoking **188**.7
heart disease
and animal research **233**.35-6
and obesity **162**.7
protective effect of alcohol **194**.18
and red meat consumption **214**.35
and smoking **188**.7
and stress **206**.4
and vegetarian diet **214**.31-2
heavy drinking *see* alcohol abuse
hens
battery farmed **233**.3, 7
genetically modified **208**.14, 37-8
hepatitis **173**.18
herbal cannabis (marijuana/grass) **186**.2, 9
herbal medicine **195**.3-4, 9, 10-13
benefits **195**.11
buying over the Internet **195**.8, 39
definition **195**.11
effectiveness of **195**.33
history of **195**.10
and the NHS **195**.11
how it works **195**.11
public attitudes to **195**.34-5
phobia treatment **206**.13
registration scheme **195**.4, 35, 38
regulation **195**.4, 33, 34-5, 36, 37-8
reporting adverse reactions **195**.38-9
safety **195**.2, 12-13, 37-9
heroin, signs of use **228**.14-15
hetero-normative attitudes **225**.11, 27
heterosexual HIV infection rate **164**.16, 17
hidden disabilities **197**.8-9
hidden homelessness **189**.4, 23
high blood pressure (hypertension) and salt intake **205**.25
high earners, attitudes to pay **227**.24-5
higher education **209**.27-39
alternatives options **185**.16-17
and business **185**.34-6
degree results and school background **209**.12
and earning power **185**.1, 21-2; **183**.34
funding **180**.28, 33; **185**.17, 35-6; **209**.2, 31-2, 35
and gender **185**.14
Government policy **185**.25
parental encouragement **209**.36
reasons for not participating **209**.27, 28
record number of applications **209**.37-8
reform **185**.20-21
and social class **209**.34-5
student life **209**.30-33

value of **185**.1, 15-17
young people's attitudes to **209**.27-8
see also further education; graduates; students
Hinduism **215**.2
and abortion **231**.19
and faith schools **215**.21
funerals **192**.35
and vegetarianism **214**.6
HIV (Human Immunodeficiency Virus) **164**.1-39
disability classification **197**.1
education **164**.18, 23-4
older people as carers **159**.5
and poverty **164**.10, 27
prevention **164**.3, 23-39
campaigns **164**.23-5
and condoms **164**.3
funding **164**.16, 39
targets **164**.28
worldwide access to prevention services **164**.39
signs and symptoms **164**.1-2
testing for **164**.2, 20-21
transmission **164**.1, 11
criminal **164**.12-13
mother-to-child **164**.3, 25, 27, 29-30, 31, 38
through blood products **164**.1, 19-20, 25
treatments **164**.2-3
antiretroviral therapy (ART) **164**.2-3, 8-9, 29, 30-32
combination therapy **164**.2-3, 8-9, 30-31
side effects **164**.3, 31
vaccines **164**.34-6
worldwide access **164**.38-9
UK statistics **164**.16, 17, 22; **173**.3, 21
and women **164**.5-6
pregnant **164**.3, 25, 27, 29-30, 31
worldwide statistics **164**.4, 38-9
and young people **164**.18; **176**.4, 28
see also AIDS
holidays
Army leave **213**.2
attitudes to **222**.2
costs **222**.5, 6-7
destinations
Britain as holiday destination **222**.2-3, 5, 11
gap year travel **222**.19
reasons for choice **222**.2-3, 11
trends **222**.1
as economic indicator **180**.5
see also responsible tourism; tourism
home building **181**.2
affordable homes **181**.6, 29
green belt land **181**.21
greenfield sites **181**.22, 26
self-build **181**.30-31
home care services **159**.4
costs **159**.26
and older people's human rights **229**.33-4
home environments and educational attainment **219**.27, 33
home information packs, political party policies **181**.23
home ownership
low-cost options **181**.25

long working hours and stress on parents **206**.22-3
    young workers **183**.28-9
    see also employment
House of Commons **175**.17-19
House of Lords **175**.18, 19-20
    and bishops **215**.6
house size, new homes **181**.15
household debt **180**.9
household waste **161**.1, 5, 6, 18-19, 31
    composition of **161**.1
    see also composting waste; waste management
households
    gender roles **221**.6
        financial **180**.18-19
    growth in numbers of **181**.2
    low-income **235**.5-8
    minimum standard income **180**.6; **235**.5
    spending **207**.7
    spending power falling **207**.8
    see also families; homeless households
houses of multiple occupation **181**.19-20
housework, and gender **221**.6
housing **181**.1-39
    and children **181**.9-11, 13, 14
    and climate change **216**.29-30
    disability rights **197**.21-2
    disabled children **197**.37
    energy efficient **235**.16
    home building **181**.2
        affordable homes **181**.6, 29
        green belt land **181**.21
        greenfield sites **181**.22, 36
        self-build **181**.30-31
    housing market as economic indicator **180**.5
    immigrants and social housing **220**.28, 29
    new homes
        lack of space **181**.15
        need for **181**.6,29
        political party policies **181**.23
    older people **159**.4
    overcrowding **181**.14
    and poverty **235**.7
    priority needs households **189**.2, 3
    problems for young people **180**.35-6; **191**.26, 27
        mental health sufferers **201**.29
    size of new houses **181**.15
    social housing *see* social housing
    and social improvement **181**.33-5
    students **185**.7
    young people **180**.35-6; **189**.24-5
    see also affordable housing; home ownership;
homelessness; rural housing;
       temporary accommodation
housing associations
    and self-build projects **181**.30, 31
    and tenants' rights to move **181**.35-6
human-animal embryos **178**.35
human cloning **211**.22-39
    arguments for and against **211**.26-7
    ethical issues **211**.8-9, 26-7
    legislation **211**.25

    therapeutic cloning **211**.9, 22-3
human embryos *see* embryos
Human Fertilisation and Embryology Bill **211**.25; **231**.2
human growth hormones (HGHs) and sport **198**.30
human reproductive cloning **211**.22, 24-7
human rights **229**.1-23
    and business **227**.27-8
    children *see* children's rights
    and corporal punishment **179**.30, 31-2
    definition **229**.1
    and Internet access **230**.38-9
    and privacy **168**.1, 3
    public attitudes to **229**.11-12
    water and sanitation **218**.32
Human Rights, Universal Declaration of
    and privacy **168**.3
Human Rights Act **229**.1-8
    arguments against **229**.7-8
    arguments for **229**.8
    coverage **229**.1-2
    and freedom of expression **196**.14
    fundamental rights and freedoms **229**.2
    and home care **229**.34
    myths **229**.3-6
    and sexual orientation **225**.7
Human Rights Risk Atlas **229**.9
human trafficking *see* trafficking
humanism **215**.4
    and embryo research **178**.36-7
    and euthanasia **217**.6
    funerals **192**.37
humour and racism **172**.11-12
hunger
    food poverty, UK **235**.17
    impact of biofuels **204**.33-4
    Millennium Development Goals **235**.26-7
    worldwide **220**.6
hunting
    for bushmeat **193**.23
    captive animals **193**.17
    endangered species **193**.1-2
hybridization **211**.2
    see also cross-contamination
hydration **205**.27-8
hydro power **204**.19, 27
hydrogen power **204**.26-7, 38
hyperactivity and food additives **205**.14-15
hypnosis **195**.4
hypomania **190**.9
hypoxia threat to ocean life **218**.24-5

I

IBRD (International Bank for Reconstruction and
Development) **226**.10
ice sheets, impact of climate change **216**.12, 15
ICSI (intracytoplasmic sperm injection) **178**.8
ICSID (International Centre for Settlement of Investment
Disputes) **226**.10

ICT
    education 230.13
    see also computers; Internet
IDA (International Development Association) 226.9
identity
    British *see* British identity
    census question 175.10-11
    and ethnicity 172.26-39
    European, young people 175.12
    national, impact of globalization 226.12
    Scottish 175.10-11, 13
identity (ID) cards 168.14-19
    benefits 168.14-16
    costs 168.17, 18-19
    problems 168.17-19
    public attitudes to 168.16
identity fraud 207.19-20; 230.24
    and ID cards 168.14-15, 18
    statistics 168.15-16
IFC (International Finance Corporation) 226.10
illegal abortion 231.12
illegal dumping *see* fly-tipping
illegal immigrants and National Identity Scheme 168.16, 18
illness, as reason for not exercising 162.31
ILO *see* International Labour Organisation
images, effects on young people's smoking 188.24-6
immigration
    attitudes to 220.22-3, 26, 27-8
    David Cameron's speech 220.30-31
    and domestic violence victims 224.37
    European Union 220.31
    and social housing 181.12; 220.28, 29
    UK 220.21-2, 24-5
    see also asylum seekers; ethnic minorities; migrant workers; migration
immune system
    and complementary therapies 195.7
    and HIV 164.1
import tariffs 226.26-7
importation of indecent articles 196.23

imprisonment *see* prison
in vitro fertilization (IVF) 178.1, 5-8, 11
    errors 178.22
    ethical dilemmas 178.17
    international comparisons 178.8
    and multiple births 178.6-7, 21-2
    and older mothers 178.17, 19-20
    statistics 178.5-6
    tagging embryos 178.22-3
    travelling abroad for 178.18, 20
    using unused embryos for research 211.31
in vitro meat 211.20-21
inactivity
    children 162.13, 15, 25
    health effects 162.11
incentives
    for health care 187.37
    for reducing waste 161.38
    for weight loss 162.22-3
incineration of waste 161.7
inclusion
    disabled children 197.36-7
        education 197.15, 27, 37
    and sport 198.18-26
    in the workforce 183.26-7
incomes
    and children's educational attainment 219.22, 23, 25
    6, 27-8, 29-30, 34
    effect on children's character 191.6
    high earners' attitudes to pay 227.24-5
    inequalities 219.8, 16; 227.15, 16
        and Internet access 230.4, 5
        see also rich-poor gap
    low-income households 235.5-8
    middle classes 219.2, 3, 9-10
    minimum standard 180.6; 235.3, 5
    minimum wage. young people 183.28
    pensioners 159.3
    perceptions of wage levels 219.15
    social housing tenants 181.35
    see also earnings; gender pay gap; salaries; wages

Vol. numbers appear first (in bold) followed by page numbers; a change in volume is preceded by a semi-colon.

Vol. 159	An Ageing Population
Vol. 161	Waste Issues
Vol. 162	Staying Fit
Vol. 164	The AIDS Crisis
Vol. 166	Marriage and Cohabitation
Vol. 168	Privacy and Surveillance
Vol. 172	Racial and Ethnic Discrimination
Vol. 173	Sexual Health
Vol. 174	Selling Sex
Vol. 175	Citizenship and Participation
Vol. 176	Health Issues for Young People
Vol. 177	Crime in the UK
Vol. 178	Reproductive Ethics
Vol. 179	Tackling Child Abuse
Vol. 180	Money and Finances
Vol. 181	The Housing Issue
Vol. 182	Teenage Conceptions
Vol. 183	Work and Employment
Vol. 184	Understanding Eating Disorders
Vol. 185	Student Matters
Vol. 186	Cannabis Use
Vol. 187	Health and the State
Vol. 188	Tobacco and Health

Vol. 189	The Homeless Population
Vol. 190	Coping with Depression
Vol. 191	The Changing Family
Vol. 192	Bereavement and Grief
Vol. 193	Endangered Species
Vol. 194	Responsible Drinking
Vol. 195	Alternative Medicine
Vol. 196	Censorship Issues
Vol. 197	Living with Disability
Vol. 198	Sport and Society
Vol. 199	Self-Harming and Suicide
Vol. 200	Sustainable Transport
Vol. 201	Mental Wellbeing
Vol. 202	Child Exploitation
Vol. 203	The Gambling Problem
Vol. 204	The Energy Crisis
Vol. 205	Nutrition and Diet
Vol. 206	Coping with Stress
Vol. 207	Consumerism and Ethics
Vol. 208	Genetic Modification
Vol. 209	Education and Society
Vol. 210	The Media
Vol. 211	Biotechnology and Cloning

Vol. 212	International Terrorism
Vol. 213	The Armed Forces
Vol. 214	Vegetarian Diets
Vol. 215	Religion in Society
Vol. 216	Tackling Climate Change
Vol. 217	Euthanasia and Assisted Suicide
Vol. 218	A Sustainable Future
Vol. 219	Class and Social Mobility
Vol. 220	Population Growth and Migration
Vol. 221	Equality and Gender Roles
Vol. 222	Tourism and Travel
Vol. 223	Crime. Punishment and Justice
Vol. 224	Domestic and Relationship Abuse
Vol. 225	LGBT Equality
Vol. 226	Globalisation and Trade
Vol. 227	Ethics in Business
Vol. 228	Illegal Drug Use
Vol. 229	Protecting Human Rights
Vol. 230	Evolution of the Internet
Vol. 231	The Abortion Debate
Vol. 232	Bullying in our Society
Vol. 233	Exploring Animal Rights
Vol. 234	Skin Deep - debating body image
Vol. 235	The Poverty Crisis

incontinence sufferers **159**.4
indecency offences **196**.22-3
independent schools
    and university applications **185**.19
independent shops **207**.28
    threat from supermarkets **207**.26, 27
indeterminate sentences **223**.20
India
    censorship of sexual content on the Internet **196**.37
    child labour **202**.11
    as gap year destination **222**.19
    gender inequality **221**.1
    impact of free trade **226**.30
indigenous people
    Amazon town ban on tourists **222**.32
    impact of tourism **222**.21-3, 29-30, 33-4
indirect discrimination
    racial **172**.4-5, 17
    and sexual orientation **225**.28
indirect euthanasia (doctrine of double effect) **217**.5, 14
Indonesia, palm oil industry and biodiversity **193**.8-9
induced pluripotent stem cells (iPS cells) **178**.38; **211**.35
    7
industry
    costs of smoking **188**.22-3
inequality
    in employment **183**.13
    and the environment **218**.3-4
    gender see gender inequality
    of global resource usage **193**.4
    health **219**.11-13
    of incomes **219**.8, 16
    schools admissions **219**.24
    and social mobility **219**.16
    UK **235**.12, 13
    see also child poverty; poverty; rich-poor gap
Infant Life Preservation Act 1929 **231**.1
infertility **178**.2-5
information
    evaluating online information 230.10-12
    online searching and gender 230.3
    patients' rights **187**.14
    personal, control of **168**.10-11, 31-2, 37; **230**.24, 30
    privacy **168**.2
    security of information and social networking **210**.30
    31
    see also Freedom of Information Act
information technology (IT) see computers; Internet
Inglis, Frances **217**.27, 29
inheritance and cohabitation **166**.15
inherited wealth **219**.8
injury as reason for not exercising **162**.32
injuries
    injured service personnel **213**.2, 7, 8-9, 10-11
    young people **176**.4
innovations of the decade **210**.17-18
insects
    declining numbers **193**.26
        bees and pollinators **193**.27-8
    effect of GM crops **208**.27
    role in ecosystems **193**.26

stag beetles, London **193**.35
instant messaging (IM)
    and bullying **232**.25
    reporting misuse **232**.36
institutional elements of marriage **166**.2-3
institutional racism **172**.1, 6-8
institutions, leaving
    as cause of homelessness **189**.6
    and help with housing **189**.25
insulin
    and biotechnology **211**.3
    and sports drug abuse **198**.30, 35
insurance and home buying **181**.24
insurance industry and climate change studies **216**.18-19
integrated healthcare **195**.23
integration
    into society **215**.9
    racial see racial integration
integrationist orientation **172**.36
intellectual impairment **197**.6
intellectual property rights see patents
intensive farming **233**.3, 7-8
inter-ethnic relationships **172**.30
interest-only mortgages **181**.28
interest rates
    annual percentage rate (APR) **180**.26
    as economic indicator **180**.5
inter-ethnic marriages see mixed-race relationships
interfaith relations, public attitudes to **212**.30-31
Intergovernmental Panel on Climate Change (IPCC)
    216.3, 5, 37
    criticism of reports **216**.22-3
internal climate variability **216**.1
International Bank for Reconstruction and Development
    (IBRD) **226**.10
International Centre for Settlement of Investment Disputes
(ICSID) **226**.10
international companies see multinational corporations
International Development Association (IDA) **226**.9
International Finance Corporation (IFC) **226**.10
International Labour Organisation (ILO) **229**.14
    and child labour **202**.2, 7-8
    definition of child labour **202**.3
    Global Action Plan **202**.7
    international labour standards **229**.14-16
    report on child labour **202**.15
International Monetary Fund (IMF) **226**.11-12
    and aid **235**.32
international parental chid abduction **166**.36
International Programme on the Elimination of Child
Labour (IPEC) **202**.7
international trade **226**.26-39
    and poverty **226**.28, 29-30, 33
    UK initiatives **226**.28
    see also free trade; globalization
international unity, need for **226**.18-19
International Women's Day **221**.36
Internet
    access devices **210**.11, 13
    addiction **230**.14, 16-17, 18
    advertising **230**.5

Vol. numbers appear first (in bold) followed by page numbers; a change in volume is preceded by a semi-**colon**.

and gender equality **215**.12
and marriage **215**.12
media portrayal **172**.38-9
public perceptions of **212**.4, 30-31
Sharia law **215**.11-12
and terrorism **212**.8-10, 32; **215**.10-11
see also Muslims
Islamic mortgages **181**.28
Islamophobia **215**.30. 31-2
and the media **215**.33
island nations, impacts of climate change **216**.16-17;
220.38
isolation
as abuse **224**.1
mental health sufferers **201**.6
older people **159**.3, 8, 17, 30
IVF *see* in vitro fertilization
IVF Witness **178**.22-3
ivory trade **193**.2, 19
IWF (Internet Watch Foundation) **196**.31, 37

J

jams, labelling rules **205**.12
Jews (Judaism) **215**.3
and abortion **231**.19
anti-semitism **215**.36
and faith schools **215**.21-2
funerals **192**.34-5
religious slaughter **233**.16
and vegetarianism **214**.6
jihad **212**.32; **215**.11
jobs
job satisfaction **183**.3-6
and population growth **220**.6
see also employment; labour market
Joffe, Lord Joel, assisted dying campaign **217**.2
Johns, Owen and Eunice **215**.25, 26; **225**.34
joints, effects of running **162**.33
journalists
female **210**.7
regulation **210**.27-8
junk food
advertising **205**.38
in children's lunchboxes **205**.10
junk mail **161**.19, 26
just-in-time Internet blocking **196**.34
justice system
and House of Lords **175**.19
see also criminal justice system
juvenile arthritis **197**.16-17
juvenile offenders and the death penalty **229**.38

K

Kenya, population growth **220**.2
kerb crawling as criminal offence **174**.2
ketamine **194**.9-10; **228**.5

'legal high' alternative **228**.6
possession, sentencing guidelines **228**.29-30
kidney problems, effect of salt intake **205**.26
Klebsiella (hospital superbug) **187**.28
knife crime **223**.5, 25, 34
discussion in schools **223**.16-17
mandatory custodial sentences **223**.21, 25
preventing **223**.34
Scotland **223**.6-7
Kosher meat **233**.16
Korsakoff's syndrome **201**.10
Krishna Avanti Hindu school **215**.21
Kyoto Protocol **216**.34, 37
and transport emissions **200**.15

L

labelling
GM food **208**.8
nanomaterials **208**.16
see also food labelling
labour market, UK **183**.16-17
decline of mid-range jobs **219**.39
fairness in jobs market **219**.18-19, 20
labour migration *see* migrant workers
lacto-ovo-vegetarians **214**.2
lacto-vegetarians **214**.2
lads' magazines **174**.29-32
age ratings **174**.28, 31
land grabs and human rights **229**.10
landfill
hazardous waste **161**.32
restoring sites to green space **161**.33
tax **161**.12, 20, 35
landlords
duties to disabled people **197**.22
reluctant **181**.17
and tenants' rights **181**.16
language
and disability
offensive language **197**.28-9
preferred terminology **197**.27
lap dancing clubs **174**.32-7
Latin America, child soldiers **202**.33
law *see* legislation
law and drugs **228**.13, 21-39
Law Lords **175**.19
law-making process **175**.18, 19
learning
effects of cannabis **186**.9-10
learning styles **209**.1-3
learning disabilities **197**.6-7, 39
causes **197**.7
definitions **197**.6-7, 39
and education **197**.14-15
and healthcare **197**.38-9
statistics **197**.7
see also disabled people
leather and vegetarianism **214**.13

leave, Army **213**.2

leaving home, young people **181**.26

Legal Aid, Sentencing and Punishment of Offenders Bill **223**.25

legal high drugs **228**.1, 36-8
    classification **228**.21
    and legislation **228**.26-7
    methoxetamine **228**.6

legal rights
    and gender equality **221**.2, 3, 35, 36
    NHS patients **187**.32-3
    young workers **183**.28-9

legalising drugs, arguments for **228**.34

legalising prostitution, effects **174**.5-7, 12-14

legislation
    and abortion **231**.1-2, 3, 32
      and disability **231**.20
    age discrimination **159**.10, 11
    and alcohol
      drink-driving **194**.31, 32
      24-hour drinking **194**.20, 21
    animal cloning **211**.11
    animal welfare **233**.1-2, 5-6
    anti-terrorism **212**.19, 20
    and assisted suicide **199**.37-8; **217**.24-38
      arguments against **217**.27
      arguments for **217**.29
      in other countries **217**.2
      in UK **217**.24-6
    and begging **189**.20
    and cannabis **186**.1-2, 4-5, 8, 9, 30-39
    and corporal punishment, European countries **179**.31
    and cyberbullying **232**.34-5, 37
    and domestic violence **224**.28-9
    drug driving **228**.26
    and drugs **176**.19; **228**.21-39
      sentencing guidelines **228**.28-31
      see also classification of drugs
    employment of young people **180**.20
    and environmental justice **218**.3, 4
    Equal Pay Act **221**.35-6

Equality Act **183**.13; **221**.3, 36

Equality Bill **172**.7, 19; **225**.6
    and euthanasia **217**.24-39
    and film classification **196**.14
    on food additives **205**.15
    food from cloned animals **211**.12
    on food labelling **205**.11-12
    and forced marriages **224**.14-15
    Gender Recognition Act **225**.6, 20, 27
    and hate crime **172**.9
    and HIV transmission **164**.14
    and homelessness **189**.1-2, 34
    human cloning **211**.25
    human rights *see* Human Rights Act
    lap dancing clubs licensing **174**.33-7
    law-making process **175**.18, 19
    and LGBT people **224**.13; **225**.6-7, 28-39
    libel law reform **210**.37
    and pornography **174**.19-20, 21-3
    on privacy **168**.2-3
    and prostitution **174**.1, 2, 3, 14, 15
      international approaches **174**.12-14
    Race Relations Act **172**.4, 16
    racial discrimination at work **172**.16-17
    and religious belief **215**.26-7; **225**.34, 35
    and sex **173**.11; **176**.21-2
      see also age of consent
    and smoking, children **176**.13
    and squatting **181**.20
    and suicide **199**.27
    and sunbeds **176**.11
    on surveillance **168**.10
    and tenants' rights **181**.16
    and work-related stress **206**.25, 28-9

leisure activities
    Middle Britain **219**.2
    older people **159**.3, 8

Lennox (dog) **233**.12-13

lesbian, gay, bisexual and transgender *see* LGBT people

lesbians
    and domestic violence **224**.5, 12-13

Vol. numbers appear first (in bold) followed by page numbers; a change in volume is preceded by a semi-**colon.**

Vol. **159** An Ageing Population
Vol. **161** Waste Issues
Vol. **162** Staying Fit
Vol. **164** The AIDS Crisis
Vol. **166** Marriage and Cohabitation
Vol. **168** Privacy and Surveillance
Vol. **172** Racial and Ethnic Discrimination
Vol. **173** Sexual Health
Vol. **174** Selling Sex
Vol. **175** Citizenship and Participation
Vol. **176** Health Issues for Young People
Vol. **177** Crime in the UK
Vol. **178** Reproductive Ethics
Vol. **179** Tackling Child Abuse
Vol. **180** Money and Finances
Vol. **181** The Housing Issue
Vol. **182** Teenage Conceptions
Vol. **183** Work and Employment
Vol. **184** Understanding Eating Disorders
Vol. **185** Student Matters
Vol. **186** Cannabis Use
Vol. **187** Health and the State
Vol. **188** Tobacco and Health

Vol. **189** The Homeless Population
Vol. **190** Coping with Depression
Vol. **191** The Changing Family
Vol. **192** Bereavement and Grief
Vol. **193** Endangered Species
Vol. **194** Responsible Drinking
Vol. **195** Alternative Medicine
Vol. **196** Censorship Issues
Vol. **197** Living with Disability
Vol. **198** Sport and Society
Vol. **199** Self-Harming and Suicide
Vol. **200** Sustainable Transport
Vol. **201** Mental Wellbeing
Vol. **202** Child Exploitation
Vol. **203** The Gambling Problem
Vol. **204** The Energy Crisis
Vol. **205** Nutrition and Diet
Vol. **206** Coping with Stress
Vol. **207** Consumerism and Ethics
Vol. **208** Genetic Modification
Vol. **209** Education and Society
Vol. **210** The Media
Vol. **211** Biotechnology and Cloning

Vol. **212** International Terrorism
Vol. **213** The Armed Forces
Vol. **214** Vegetarian Diets
Vol. **215** Religion in Society
Vol. **216** Tackling Climate Change
Vol. **217** Euthanasia and Assisted Suicide
Vol. **218** A Sustainable Future
Vol. **219** Class and Social Mobility
Vol. **220** Population Growth and Migration
Vol. **221** Equality and Gender Roles
Vol. **222** Tourism and Travel
Vol. **223** Crime, Punishment and Justice
Vol. **224** Domestic and Relationship Abuse
Vol. **225** LGBT Equality
Vol. **226** Globalisation and Trade
Vol. **227** Ethics in Business
Vol. **228** Illegal Drug Use
Vol. **229** Protecting Human Rights
Vol. **230** Evolution of the Internet
Vol. **231** The Abortion Debate
Vol. **232** Bullying in our Society
Vol. **233** Exploring Animal Rights
Vol. **234** Skin Deep - debating body image
Vol. **235** The Poverty Crisis

having children **178**.9-10
human rights **229**.31-2
young people, mental health problems **201**.3
see also homosexuality; same-sex relationships
Lewy bodies (dementia) **201**.10
LGBT people **225**.1-39
attitudes to **225**.11-13
equality policies, EU **225**.12-13
and the law **225**.28-39
and schools **225**.5-8
and social exclusion **225**.9
transgender issues **225**.19-27
see also gay men; lesbians; same-sex relationships; sexual
orientation
libel
libel actions, celebrities **210**.38
libel laws reform **210**.37
liberalization of trade   *see* free trade
licence periods (prison sentences) **223**.19-20, 21
Licensing Act and lap dancing clubs **174**.33-7
licensing hours
24-hour licensing **194**.20
and crime **194**.21
life expectancy **159**.6
and obesity **176**.7
HIV patients **164**.8-9
and population growth prediction **220**.9
and poverty **219**.13
and smoking **188**.18
and social class **188**.18
ways of increasing **159**.32-4
UK **159**.3, 34
life insurance cover and home buying **181**.24
life peers **175**.19
life sentences **223**.20, 21
lifestyle
and ageing **159**.2, 34
and depression **190**.3
and health **219**.12
and life expectancy **159**.33-4
middle classes **219**.1-2, 9-10
and stress **206**.18, 32-4
students **209**.30-33
and weight loss **162**.20
lifetime debt **180**.11-12
light bulbs, recycling **161**.24
light rail **200**.30, 33-4
light therapy for Seasonal Affective Disorder **190**.6-7
lignocellulose **204**.32
literacy, women, worldwide **221**.37
litter **161**.15-16, 21
liver damage and alcohol **194**.6
Livewell menu **214**.22-3
living funerals **192**.36
living wage for garment industry workers **229**.13
living wills *see* advance directives (living wills)
Lloyds Banking Group, charitable work **227**.20
loans **180**.27; **235**.11-12
to entrepreneurs in developing countries **235**.33
student **180**.28, 33; **185**.2
see also credit; debt

local authorities
duty to house **189**.1-2, 34
and ending violence against women and girls **224**.29
and greenfield development **181**.22
and housing young people **181**.26-7
responsibilities for under 16s **224**.37
and self-build projects **181**.30
and social housing **181**.29
and surveillance **168**.20-21
see also council tenants
local communities, effects of tourism **222**.21-3, 29-30, 33-4
Local Safeguarding Children's Boards **224**.37
lodgers' rights **181**.16
logbook loans **235**.12
logging, effect on wildlife **193**.4
London
bombings **212**.4, 5
congestion charge **200**.17-18
hostels for homeless people **189**.35
Olympics
and sex trafficking **229**.20
and tourism **222**.12-13
public transport **200**.30
rare wildlife species **193**.35
rough sleepers **189**.16
underground travel, disabled people **197**.12
loneliness
after divorce **166**.23
older people **159**.3, 8, 17, 30
and stress **206**.18
long-term illness **159**.4
Lord Speaker **175**.20
losing weight *see* weight loss
lotteries **203**.4
see also National Lottery
Lovelock, James **220**.12
low-cost home ownership **181**.25
low income countries **235**.28-30
low income households **235**.5-8
see also child poverty
low income threshold **235**.5
low pay **235**.6
low-tar cigarettes **188**.7, 10
loyalty cards and personal data **168**.8
lung cancer
and cannabis use **186**.15, 16
and smoking, **188**.6, 8
lung damage
through cannabis use **186**.28
through smoking **188**.5
Luxembourg, assisted dying legislation **217**.2
lynx, reintroduction into Britain **193**.33, 34
Lynx deodorant, advertisements **234**.22

M

M4 bus lane **200**.36
macrobiotic diets **195**.4-5
magazines

airbrushing in *Healthy* magazine **234**.27-8

diversity award **234**.38

influence on young people smoking **188**.25-6

teenage magazines and sexualisation of children **174**.39

UK magazine sector **210**.2-3

Vogue and body image **234**.5-6

see also lads' magazines

magnetic resonance imaging (MRI) as alternative to animal research **233**.32

maintained faith schools **209**.22-3

major (clinical) depression **190**.2, 21

Maldives

impact of sea level rise **220**.38

impact of tourism **222**.23

malnutrition **176**.4

see also hunger

Management of Health and Safety at Work Regulations, and stress **206**.25, 28

Management Standards, work-related stress **206**.25-6

management

gender gap **221**.19-20

glass ceiling **221**.21-2

mandatory eviction **181**.16

mandatory life sentences **223**.21

mania **190**.8, 21

manic depression *see* bipolar affective disorder

manifestos, political **175**.26

Maplecroft Human Rights Risk Atlas **229**.9

mapping genes **208**.13

margin of appreciation, European Court of Human Rights **229**.6

marijuana *see* herbal cannabis

Marine and Coastal Access Act **218**.22

marine environments

acidification **193**.30

impacts of tourism **222**.25

protection **218**.22-3

threats to **218**.24-5

Marine Strategy Framework Directive **218**.22

marital status

and health **166**.15

and smoking **188**.1

marmalade, labelling rules **205**.12

marriage **166**.1-20

age at **166**.4, 6

arranged marriages **166**.16

attitudes to **166**.1-2, 7, 9-11

child marriage **202**.19

and civil partnerships **225**.35

'common law' marriage **166**.12

expectations of cohabiting partners **166**.2, 7

financial incentives **166**.5; **191**.2

forced marriages **166**.17-20; **224**.3, 14-15, 36-7

and Islam **215**.12

institutional elements **166**.2-3

and Islam **215**.12

male and female attitudes to **166**.3

reasons for marrying **166**.2

reasons for not marrying **166**.2, 9-11

relational elements **166**.2-3

same-sex couples **225**.33

statistics **166**.4, 6; **191**.1, 3

and stepfamilies *see* stepfamilies

and transsexuals **225**.27

trends **191**.1-4

unhappy **166**.7-8

mass surveillance **168**.6

masturbation **173**.2

maternity leave **183**.18, 21, 23, 24; **191**.37-8

effect on businesses **183**.23

maternity pay **191**.38

maternity rights **191**.37-8

maturity as a factor in sentencing young people **223**.33-4

Maudsley Model treatment programme **184**.29-30

Mayhew Animal Home **233**.1

MBCT (mindfulness-based cognitive therapy) **190**.34-6

MDMA *see* ecstasy

meat consumption

bushmeat trade **193**.23

meat substitutes **214**.9, 11

need to reduce **214**.15-16, 22-3, 24, 27

Vol. numbers appear first (in bold) followed by page numbers; a change in volume is preceded by a semi-**colon.**

Vol. 159 An Ageing Population	**Vol. 189** The Homeless Population
Vol. 161 Waste Issues	**Vol. 190** Coping with Depression
Vol. 162 Staying Fit	**Vol. 191** The Changing Family
Vol. 164 The AIDS Crisis	**Vol. 192** Bereavement and Grief
Vol. 166 Marriage and Cohabitation	**Vol. 193** Endangered Species
Vol. 168 Privacy and Surveillance	**Vol. 194** Responsible Drinking
Vol. 172 Racial and Ethnic Discrimination	**Vol. 195** Alternative Medicine
Vol. 173 Sexual Health	**Vol. 196** Censorship Issues
Vol. 174 Selling Sex	**Vol. 197** Living with Disability
Vol. 175 Citizenship and Participation	**Vol. 198** Sport and Society
Vol. 176 Health Issues for Young People	**Vol. 199** Self-Harming and Suicide
Vol. 177 Crime in the UK	**Vol. 200** Sustainable Transport
Vol. 178 Reproductive Ethics	**Vol. 201** Mental Wellbeing
Vol. 179 Tackling Child Abuse	**Vol. 202** Child Exploitation
Vol. 180 Money and Finances	**Vol. 203** The Gambling Problem
Vol. 181 The Housing Issue	**Vol. 204** The Energy Crisis
Vol. 182 Teenage Conceptions	**Vol. 205** Nutrition and Diet
Vol. 183 Work and Employment	**Vol. 206** Coping with Stress
Vol. 184 Understanding Eating Disorders	**Vol. 207** Consumerism and Ethics
Vol. 185 Student Matters	**Vol. 208** Genetic Modification
Vol. 186 Cannabis Use	**Vol. 209** Education and Society
Vol. 187 Health and the State	**Vol. 210** The Media
Vol. 188 Tobacco and Health	**Vol. 211** Biotechnology and Cloning

Vol. 212 International Terrorism
Vol. 213 The Armed Forces
Vol. 214 Vegetarian Diets
Vol. 215 Religion in Society
Vol. 216 Tackling Climate Change
Vol. 217 Euthanasia and Assisted Suicide
Vol. 218 A Sustainable Future
Vol. 219 Class and Social Mobility
Vol. 220 Population Growth and Migration
Vol. 221 Equality and Gender Roles
Vol. 222 Tourism and Travel
Vol. 223 Crime, Punishment and Justice
Vol. 224 Domestic and Relationship Abuse
Vol. 225 LGBT Equality
Vol. 226 Globalisation and Trade
Vol. 227 Ethics in Business
Vol. 228 Illegal Drug Use
Vol. 229 Protecting Human Rights
Vol. 230 Evolution of the Internet
Vol. 231 The Abortion Debate
Vol. 232 Bullying in our Society
Vol. 233 Exploring Animal Rights
Vol. 234 Skin Deep - debating body image
Vol. 235 The Poverty Crisis

nutrients **205**.3; **214**.34-5
    red meat and health **214**.34-5
meat free foods **214**.7-8
Meat Free Mondays campaign **214**.27
meat production
    arguments for and against **214**.18-21
    from cloned cows **211**.12, 15-17
    and the environment **214**.16, 17, 18-19, 20-21
    intensively farming **233**.3, 7-8
    laboratory-grown meat **211**.20-21
    large-scale pig farms **233**.11
    product labelling rules **205**.11
    sustainable **214**.14, 20-21, 23
media **210**.1-39
    and attitudes to Europe **175**.12
    and body image **184**.23-4; **234**.5, 7, 8, 10, 11, 18
        men **184**.13
    climate change reporting **216**.22-4
    drug death reporting **186**.32-3
    fuelling racism **172**.2, 10
    and gambling **203**.26
    influence on young people smoking **188**.25-6
    and Islamophobia **215**.33
    and mental ill health **201**.23
    multi-tasking **210**.11
    and Muslims **172**.38-9
    new technologies **210**.13-26
    and the permissive society **196**.25-6
    political coverage and young people **175**.31-2
    and privacy **168**.7, 28-9; **210**.33-9
    public opinion on media freedom **229**.12
    and racist remarks **172**.11-12
    regulation **210**.27-9, 34
    and religion **215**.13
    and suicide **199**.35, 36
    trends **210**.1-12
    violence *see* violence, media
    WikiLeaks **210**.20-26
    see also broadcasters; films; Internet; magazines;
newspapers; press; radio; telecommunications; television
mediation and divorce **166**.26, 35, 38-9
medical abortion **231**.7
medical ethics argument against euthanasia **217**.4
medical insurance **187**.24
medical model of disability **197**.2
medical profession
    and assisted suicide **217**.22, 24-5
    effects of legalizing assisted dying **217**.4, 8, 11, 31
    see also doctors
medical research, use of animals **233**.28-39
medical treatment
    injured service personnel **213**.2, 8-9, 10-11
    for obesity **162**.2-3, 6
    patient's right to refuse **217**.13, 25
    withdrawing **217**.14
    see also palliative care
medical waste disposal **161**.24
medically-assisted dying *see* physician-assisted suicide
medicinal drug use, cannabis **186**.8, 16-17
medicines
    assessment for NHS use **187**.22-3

consumer buying habits **195**.8
    Internet purchasing **195**.8, 39
    effects on fertility **178**.4, 5
    from GM plants **208**.21-2
    from GM animals **208**.13
    labelling of additives **205**.16
    for stress and anxiety **206**.3, 13
    see also drug treatments, drugs
meditation as treatment for depression **190**.34-6; **195**.15
mega-farms **233**.9-11
melanoma **176**.10-11
Members of Parliament *see* MPs
memorial websites **192**.38-9
memories of the deceased *see* remembrance of the deceased
men
    and abortion **231**.9
    and alcohol limits **194**.14
    body image concerns **234**.13, 16-17
    career aspirations **221**.21
    and compulsive shopping **207**.6
    as domestic abuse victims **224**.5, 9-10, 11
    and eating disorders **184**.11-12, 13, 20
    fertility problems **178**.3, 4-5, 8
    and household financial roles **180**.18-19
    and household tasks **221**.6
    Internet usage **230**.3-4
    marriage expectations **166**.3
    media usage **210**.12
    and mental health problems **190**.18-19
    parenting roles **191**.30-33
    paternity leave **221**.4-5
    paternity rights **191**.39
    post-natal depression **190**.16-17
    and smoking **188**.1, 15
    and suicide **199**.21, 28
    symptoms of stress **206**.7-8
    see also boys and young men; fathers; gay men
Mencap **197**.39
Mental Capacity Act and right to refuse medical treatment **217**.13
mental health **176**.4, 29-39
    and abortion **231**.14-15
    and alcohol **194**.6
    awareness of **176**.31-2
    benefits of exercise **162**.37, 38
    and body image **234**.10, 11, 19
    and cannabis **186**.10-13, 16, 28-9, 30, 31, 32; **228**.8
    children **176**.29-30; 36-7
        and aggression **224**.23
    definition **201**.33, 35
    and homeless people **189**.9-11
    improving **201**.33-4, 35-6
    and older people **159**.4
        see also dementia
    risk factors **176**.29
    statistics, young people **190**.27
    and stress **206**.36-7
    strategies **201**.5, 35
    students **185**.8
    treatment **176**.30
    young people **176**.4, 29-39; **190**.27

see also dementia; depression
Mental Health Act **201**.38-9
    'nearest relative' powers **190**.11
mental health services **201**.5
    insufficiencies **201**.37
    and young people **201**.10-11, 36
mental health trusts **187**.6
mental illness **201**.1-39
    and Armed Forces personnel **213**.3-4, 5, 6
    attitudes to **201**.22-3, 31
    and cannabis **228**.8
    causes **201**.32-3
    children **201**.2-4
    costs **201**.1, 23
    and domestic violence **224**.7
    ex-service personnel **213**.33-4
    and gambling **203**.37
    and homosexuality **201**.3
    prevalence **201**.5, 6
    and self-harm **199**.2
    and social welfare problems **201**.29
    stigma **201**.22-3, 31
      self-stigma **201**.28
      young carers **201**.8
    and suicide **199**.21, 24
    young people **201**.2-4, 7, 29-30
    see also bipolar affective disorder; dementia; depression;
post-traumatic stress disorder; schizophrenia
mental symptoms
    of anxiety **206**.10
    of stress **206**.1-2, 9, 19
mentoring
    of girls **221**.32
    of young people by ex-service personnel **213**.32
mephedrone (meow meow) **228**.23, 36, 37
    classification **228**.21-2, 23, 32
mercy killing see non-voluntary euthanasia
metabolic syndrome and vegetarianism **214**.31-2
metals recycling **161**.24
    aluminium **161**.22, 27
methamphetamine (crystal meth) **228**.23

methane
    as car fuel **204**.39
    emissions from biodegradable products **218**.37
Methodist Church and abortion **231**.19
methoxetamine (MXE/Mexxy) **228**.6
metro systems **200**.34
Metropolitan Police **172**.7-8
microdosing as alternative to animal research **233**.32
microfinance **235**.34-5
microgeneration of energy **204**.35-6
    solar water heating **204**.21-2
    water power **204**.19
middle-classes **219**.1-2, 9-10
Middle East
    child soldiers **202**.33
    criminalization of homosexuality **225**.39
    press freedom **196**.2
    as tourist destination **222**.8
middle-income countries **235**.28-30
midwives, religious objection to abortion **231**.30
migrant workers **220**.32-3
    returning due to unemployment **220**.34
    women **174**.17-18; **220**.35
migration **220**.8-9, 20-39
    and climate change **220**.38, 39
    elimination of barriers, economic benefits **226**.39
    forced **220**.36-7
    and population growth **220**.9
    reasons for **220**.20, 36-7
    statistics **220**.21
    to UK **220**.20-21, 24-5
    of workforce (brain drain) **220**.32-3
    see also asylum seekers; immigration
military forces, USA, and sexual orientation **225**.38-9
milk
    from cloned cows **211**.12, 13-14
    and balanced diet **205**.3, 28
    labelling of milk products **205**.11
Millennium Development Goals **226**.3; 1-2, 25-7
    2011 report **218**.39
    education **229**.27-8

Vol. numbers appear first (in bold) followed by page numbers; a change in volume is preceded by a semi-**colon**.

Vol. 159 An Ageing Population	**Vol. 189** The Homeless Population	**Vol. 212** International Terrorism
Vol. 161 Waste Issues	**Vol. 190** Coping with Depression	**Vol. 213** The Armed Forces
Vol. 162 Staying Fit	**Vol. 191** The Changing Family	**Vol. 214** Vegetarian Diets
Vol. 164 The AIDS Crisis	**Vol. 192** Bereavement and Grief	**Vol. 215** Religion in Society
Vol. 166 Marriage and Cohabitation	**Vol. 193** Endangered Species	**Vol. 216** Tackling Climate Change
Vol. 168 Privacy and Surveillance	**Vol. 194** Responsible Drinking	**Vol. 217** Euthanasia and Assisted Suicide
Vol. 172 Racial and Ethnic Discrimination	**Vol. 195** Alternative Medicine	**Vol. 218** A Sustainable Future
Vol. 173 Sexual Health	**Vol. 196** Censorship Issues	**Vol. 219** Class and Social Mobility
Vol. 174 Selling Sex	**Vol. 197** Living with Disability	**Vol. 220** Population Growth and Migration
Vol. 175 Citizenship and Participation	**Vol. 198** Sport and Society	**Vol. 221** Equality and Gender Roles
Vol. 176 Health Issues for Young People	**Vol. 199** Self-Harming and Suicide	**Vol. 222** Tourism and Travel
Vol. 177 Crime in the UK	**Vol. 200** Sustainable Transport	**Vol. 223** Crime. Punishment and Justice
Vol. 178 Reproductive Ethics	**Vol. 201** Mental Wellbeing	**Vol. 224** Domestic and Relationship Abuse
Vol. 179 Tackling Child Abuse	**Vol. 202** Child Exploitation	**Vol. 225** LGBT Equality
Vol. 180 Money and Finances	**Vol. 203** The Gambling Problem	**Vol. 226** Globalisation and Trade
Vol. 181 The Housing Issue	**Vol. 204** The Energy Crisis	**Vol. 227** Ethics in Business
Vol. 182 Teenage Conceptions	**Vol. 205** Nutrition and Diet	**Vol. 228** Illegal Drug Use
Vol. 183 Work and Employment	**Vol. 206** Coping with Stress	**Vol. 229** Protecting Human Rights
Vol. 184 Understanding Eating Disorders	**Vol. 207** Consumerism and Ethics	**Vol. 230** Evolution of the Internet
Vol. 185 Student Matters	**Vol. 208** Genetic Modification	**Vol. 231** The Abortion Debate
Vol. 186 Cannabis Use	**Vol. 209** Education and Society	**Vol. 232** Bullying in our Society
Vol. 187 Health and the State	**Vol. 210** The Media	**Vol. 233** Exploring Animal Rights
Vol. 188 Tobacco and Health	**Vol. 211** Biotechnology and Cloning	**Vol. 234** Skin Deep - debating body image
		Vol. 235 The Poverty Crisis

employment **235**.26
hunger **235**.26-7
poverty reduction **235**.25-6
water and sanitation **218**.31, 36-7
mindfulness-based cognitive therapy (MBCT) **190**.34-6
minimum income standard **180**.6; **235**.3, 5
minimum pricing, alcohol **194**.36, 37
minimum wage, young workers **183**.28
Ministers, Government **175**.17, 20
minority ethnic groups *see* ethnic minorities
minority rights **229**.24-39
miscegenation *see* mixed-race relationships
Misuse of Drugs Act 1971 **228**.21, 22, 24
sentencing guidelines **228**.28-31
mixed-race identity **172**.31-3
mixed-race relationships **172**.30
mobile phones
and blogging **210**.16
bullying by **232**.17, 25, 27, 29
information logging **168**.8
and Internet access **230**.1
and relationship abuse **224**.20
and social networking **210**.14
usage trends **210**.11
and gender **210**.12
international comparison **210**.13-14
modelling
model dies of anorexia **234**.36
teenagers **234**.35
models of disability **197**.2
monarchy, role in government **175**.20
money
British currency **175**.2
financial abuse **159**.16
money management **180**.7-19
students **180**.28-9, 32-3; **185**.2-3, 11
worries
and depression **190**.5
and stress **206**.18, 21, 39
see also banks; credit; debt; incomes; wages
Mongolia, education programme **229**.28
monoamine oxidase inhibitors (MAOIs) **190**.11, 33
Monsanto **208**.3-4
mood changes as sign of eating disorders **184**.30
mood stabilising drugs **190**.10
moral rights of embryos **178**.33-4; **211**.31, 34
morality and business **227**.22-3
morning after pill *see* emergency contraception
mortality
Armed Forces mortality rate **213**.9
and depression **190**.20
and population trends **220**.9
see also life expectancy
mortgages **181**.24, 28
lifetime mortgages **180**.23
mosques as targets of hate crime **215**.29
motherhood role and the abortion debate **231**.18-19
mothers
in the Army **213**.13-14
dieting, effect on daughters **184**.21-2
effect on children's body image **184**.21-2

girl soldiers **202**.36
HIV transmission to children **164**.3, 25, 27, 29-30, 31, 38
maternity rights **191**.37-8
as migrant workers **220**.35
and pay gap **221**.24
preferring not to work **183**.25
stay-at-home mothers suffering stress **191**.35
see also working mothers
motoring
and disability **197**.11
see also cars; driving
motorways
M4 bus lane **200**.36
motorway phobia **200**.4
motorway travel frequency **200**.5
mourning *see* grief
movies *see* films
MPs **175**.17, 26
communicating with **175**.25, 35
and the drugs debate **186**.34-5
electing **175**.22-9
female **221**.13, 15, 20
term limit proposal **175**.21
MRI (magnetic resonance imaging) as alternative to animal research **233**.32
MRSA **187**.28, 29
MSSA **187**.28
multiculturalism **172**.26-8
in schools **172**.36-7
multinational corporations (MNCs) **226**.1, 27
and tax **227**.32-3
multiple births and IVF **178**.6-7
health problems **178**.21-2
multiple embryo transfers **178**.8
multiple sclerosis (MS)
classification as disability **197**.1
stem cell treatment **211**.38-9
muscular dystrophies **197**.3
Muslims **172**.2
anti-Muslim hate crime **215**.28-30
British **215**.9-12
discrimination against **215**.30, 31-2
migrants' experiences of life in Britain **172**.35
Muslim extremists, protests against British soldiers **196**.9-10
public attitudes to **212**.4, 30-31; **215**.33
ritual slaughter **233**.16
as stop and search targets **212**.28-9
veiling of Muslim women **215**.34-8
see also Islam
MXE (methoxetamine) **228**.6
Myanmar, forced labour **229**.15
MyMoney education project **180**.38
MySpace, reporting inappropriate content **232**.35

N

name-calling, dealing with **232**.19-20

nanotechnology **208**.15-16
National Crime Agency **223**.22
National DNA Database **168**.7, 11-12
National Health Service *see* NHS
national identity
    British *see* British identity
    cards *see* identity cards
    census question **175**.10-11
    and globalization **226**.12
    Scottish **175**.10-11, 13
National Identity Scheme **168**.14-19
National Institute for Clinical Excellence (NICE) *see* NICE
National Lottery
    children participating **203**.12-13
    disability sports funding **198**.18
    online participation **203**.4
National Patient Safety Agency (NPSA) **187**.6
national symbols, British **175**.2
natural family planning **182**.19
natural gas, industry trends **204**.1
natural medicine *see* complementary medicine (CM)
natural resources consumption **218**.7-8, 13-14
    impact of global development **226**.3-4
    impact of tourism **222**.29
    water **218**.33
Nazareth, Colombia, ban on tourists **222**.32
nearest relative under Mental Health Act **190**.11; **201**.38-9
NEETs (young people not in employment, education or training) **183**.32
negative body image see body image, negative
neglect
    children **179**.3
        reporting **179**.7
        signs **179**.5
        taking children into care **179**.10-11
        trafficked children **202**.29
    older people **159**.17
Netherlands, The
    assisted dying legislation **217**.2, 9, 11

elderly people's fears of euthanasia **217**.33
    LGBT equality policy **225**.13
    regulation of prostitution **174**.12-13
    sex education **182**.28-9, 32-4
neurobiology and sexual orientation **225**.15-16
news media and women **210**.6-8
    female presenters and reporters **210**.7
    women as news subjects **210**.6, 7-8
News of the World, phone-hacking **210**.35-6
newspapers **210**.1-2
    ownership **210**.2
    paid-for websites **210**.19
    regulations **210**.27-8
NGOs (non-governmental organisations) **226**.1, 4
NHS (National Health Service) **187**.1-23; **219**.12
    achievements **187**.25-6
    anti-smoking strategies, pregnant women **188**.30-32
    constitution **187**.12-15
    costs of smoking **188**.22
    criticisms of **187**.26
        by US politicans **187**.19-20
    disability discrimination **197**.30, 38-9
    and eating disorders **184**.36
    funding **187**.1, 3, 25, 26, 30
        patients' views **187**.11-12, 16-17
    future proposals **187**.32-9
    and herbal medicine **195**.11
    and homeopathy **195**.16, 17-22, 24-5
    international comparisons **187**.4, 20-21
    and older people **159**.4
    patients' views **187**.11-12, 16-17
    patients with learning difficulties **197**.38-9
    performance **187**.1, 20-21
    post traumatic stress disorder treatment **213**.3-4
    problems **187**.25-31
    quality of care **187**.4, 26-8
    reform strategy **187**.38-9
    self-harm treatment **199**.13-14, 15, 18
    size **187**.1, 3
    statistics **187**.1, 3, 5-6
    waiting times **187**.20-21

Vol. numbers appear first (in bold) followed by page numbers; a change in volume is preceded by a semi-**colon.**

Vol. 159   An Ageing Population
Vol. 161   Waste Issues
Vol. 162   Staying Fit
Vol. 164   The AIDS Crisis
Vol. 166   Marriage and Cohabitation
Vol. 168   Privacy and Surveillance
Vol. 172   Racial and Ethnic Discrimination
Vol. 173   Sexual Health
Vol. 174   Selling Sex
Vol. 175   Citizenship and Participation
Vol. 176   Health Issues for Young People
Vol. 177   Crime in the UK
Vol. 178   Reproductive Ethics
Vol. 179   Tackling Child Abuse
Vol. 180   Money and Finances
Vol. 181   The Housing Issue
Vol. 182   Teenage Conceptions
Vol. 183   Work and Employment
Vol. 184   Understanding Eating Disorders
Vol. 185   Student Matters
Vol. 186   Cannabis Use
Vol. 187   Health and the State
Vol. 188   Tobacco and Health

Vol. 189   The Homeless Population
Vol. 190   Coping with Depression
Vol. 191   The Changing Family
Vol. 192   Bereavement and Grief
Vol. 193   Endangered Species
Vol. 194   Responsible Drinking
Vol. 195   Alternative Medicine
Vol. 196   Censorship Issues
Vol. 197   Living with Disability
Vol. 198   Sport and Society
Vol. 199   Self-Harming and Suicide
Vol. 200   Sustainable Transport
Vol. 201   Mental Wellbeing
Vol. 202   Child Exploitation
Vol. 203   The Gambling Problem
Vol. 204   The Energy Crisis
Vol. 205   Nutrition and Diet
Vol. 206   Coping with Stress
Vol. 207   Consumerism and Ethics
Vol. 208   Genetic Modification
Vol. 209   Education and Society
Vol. 210   The Media
Vol. 211   Biotechnology and Cloning

Vol. 212   International Terrorism
Vol. 213   The Armed Forces
Vol. 214   Vegetarian Diets
Vol. 215   Religion in Society
Vol. 216   Tackling Climate Change
Vol. 217   Euthanasia and Assisted Suicide
Vol. 218   A Sustainable Future
Vol. 219   Class and Social Mobility
Vol. 220   Population Growth and Migration
Vol. 221   Equality and Gender Roles
Vol. 222   Tourism and Travel
Vol. 223   Crime. Punishment and Justice
Vol. 224   Domestic and Relationship Abuse
Vol. 225   LGBT Equality
Vol. 226   Globalisation and Trade
Vol. 227   Ethics in Business
Vol. 228   Illegal Drug Use
Vol. 229   Protecting Human Rights
Vol. 230   Evolution of the Internet
Vol. 231   The Abortion Debate
Vol. 232   Bullying in our Society
Vol. 233   Exploring Animal Rights
Vol. 234   Skin Deep - debating body image
Vol. 235   The Poverty Crisis

workforce **187**.2, 3
nicotine
    addiction **188**.10, 16
        effects on heart **188**.7
        poisoning, tobacco pickers **188**.39
nicotine replacement therapies **188**.6
        VAT on **188**.23
night eating syndrome **184**.8
night shelters *see* hostels for homeless people
Nimrod aircraft contract cancellation **213**.21
niqab, arguments for and against wearing **215**.37-8
noise
    from traffic **200**.14-15, 22
    from wind turbines **204**.12
non-agricultural market access (NAMA) **226**.15-16
non-governmental organisations (NGOs) **226**.1, 4
non-native species, impact of **193**.12
    UK **193**.38-9
non-reproductive cloning *see* therapeutic cloning
non-voluntary euthanasia **217**.5
    Kay Inglis **217**.27, 29
North Korea, death penalty **229**.37
Northern Ireland
    abortion law **231**.3, 25
    drug strategy **228**.24
    homelessness **189**.4
    Northern Ireland Assembly, submitting a petition **175**.35
    Republican terrorist groups **212**.14
Northern Rock and the banking crisis **180**.4
novel foods **211**.17
Novel Foods Regulation and clonng **211**.12
novel psychoactive substances *see* legal high drugs
NSPCC **179**.14
    and ChildLine **179**.13
nuclear power **204**.26
    political support for **216**.25
number plate recognition **168**.9
nurses, to have degree qualification **187**.33-5
nutrition
    and ageing **159**.2
    and food groups **205**.2-3, 4-5
    and GM crops **208**.35-6
    and meat **214**.34-5
    nutrition labelling **205**.13
    organic produce **205**.36
    Quorn products **214**.9
    teenagers **176**.8-9
    and veganism **214**.3
    and vegetarianism **214**.28-39
    see also diet; healthy eating

Obama, Barack, and closure of Guantánamo Bay **212**.33, 34-5
obesity **162**.1-10; **205**.19-21
    and alcohol **194**.18
    avoidance *see* weight management
    and Body Mass Index (BMI) **162**.1, 4, 5, 23
    causes **162**.2, 5, 8
    in children *see* childhood obesity
    definitions **162**.1, 4
    discrimination **162**.21
    government strategies **162**.4-5, 9-10, 17-18, 22-3; **205**.20-21
        potential harm **184**.33
    and health **162**.1-2, 5, 6, 7, 19, 25; **176**.7
    and life expectancy **176**.7
    measurement **162**.1
    predictions **162**.10, 18, 19
    and salt intake **205**.26
    statistics **162**.1, 5, 6, 7, 18; **187**.4
    treatment **162**.2-3, 6, 20
    in the workplace **162**.21
    worldwide **162**.7
    and young people **176**.2, 3, 7, 9
    see also body weight; weight management
Obscene Publications Acts **174**.21; **196**.14, 22
obscenity **196**.22-3
obsession with food **184**.9-11
oceans
    acidification **193**.30
    threats to **218**.24-5
occupational segregation **221**.19, 27-9
occupational therapists **197**.4
Ofcom **196**.18-20
    Broadcasting Code **210**.27
    and offensive language on television **196**.21, 24
Offences against the Person Act 1861 **231**.1
Offender Discrimination Act **223**.27
offenders
    recovery programmes **223**.23-4
    and restorative justice **223**.28-9
    see also ex-offenders
offensive language
    and disabled people **197**.28-9
    on television **196**.21, 24
offensive material
    broadcasters' rights **196**.24
    cartoons in airport prayer room **196**.11-12
Official Opposition **175**.17, 19
offsetting carbon *see* carbon offsetting
offshore wind power **204**.14-18
Ofsted and sexuality equality legislation **225**.7
oil
    arguments against production **204**.9-10
    industry trends **204**.1
    recycling **161**.5, 23, 28
older people
    abuse of **159**.4, 6, 16-18
    as carers **159**.4, 5
    communications trends **210**.11-12
    and health **159**.4, 6, 8, 35-9
    home care and human rights **229**.33-4
    in employment **159**.10, 15
    Internet usage **230**.5, 19-21
    and poverty **235**.6, 8
    spending **159**.19
    and suicide **199**.20, 21

worldwide **159**.5, 6

UK **159**.3-4, 7-8

older women

    and eating disorders **184**.14-15

    and IVF **178**.17, 19-20

older workers **159**.10, 15; **183**.15, 27

    and age discrimination **159**.4, 8-13

Olympic Games

    gender equality **198**.19

    London, opening ceremony, use of animals **233**.13

    and sex trafficking **229**.20

    and sports competition for young people **198**.5

    talent identification **198**.8-10

    and tourist industry **222**.12-13

    see also Paralympic Games

omega 3 fatty acids **214**.29, 33

one-child rule, China **220**.4, 18

one-parent families *see* lone parents

online bullying *see* cyberbullying

online child sexual abuse **179**.15-16, 17

online divorces **166**.27

online gambling **203**.28-9

    participation rates **203**.4

    women **203**.35-6

    young people **203**.16-18

online grooming **179**.16; **230**.23-4

online reputation **230**.31-2

online retail *see* Internet shopping

online safety, social networking **179**.18

online surveillance **168**.13-14, 32-3

online testing for chlamydia **173**.28

online travel booking **222**.3

Opposition parties **175**.17, 19

Orbach, Susie **234**.5, 7-8

Oregon State, assisted dying legislation **217**.2, 11

organ donation **192**.28

    from euthanasia victims **217**.32

    and HIV transmission **164**.1

organ harvesting and human trafficking **229**.18

organ transplants *see* therapeutic cloning

organic farming

and the environment **205**.34, 35

and food safety **205**.34, 36

organic food **205**.30, 33, 34-6; **214**.23, 29

    arguments against **205**.34

    arguments for **205**.35-6

    consumer attitudes **207**.30

organic waste

    composting **161**.19, 28-9, 30

    energy generation **204**.6

    gas production **204**.24

Origin Assured fur assurance scheme **233**.19

orphans, AIDS **164**.6-7

orthorexia nervosa **184**.9

osteoporosis

    and cannabis use **186**.6

    effect of salt intake **205**.25-6

outsourcing of Internet control **196**.33-4

overall poverty **235**.1

overdoses *see* drug overdoses

overdrafts **180**.26-7

overseas burial **192**.31

overseas travel, attitudes to **222**.2

    see also tourism

overweight people *see* obesity

ovo-vegetarians **214**.2

ovulation disorders **178**.4

ownership, newspapers **210**.2

Oxbridge

    entrance tests **185**.23

    teachers' misconceptions about **185**.24

oxygen transfer enhancement **198**.29

P

packaging waste **161**.4, 5, 12

packed lunches, children **205**.7, 10

paedophiles

    disclosure of **179**.20-21

    help for **179**.22-3

    see also child pornography; sex offenders

Vol. numbers appear first (in bold) followed by page numbers; a change in volume is preceded by a semi-**colon**.

Vol. 159 An Ageing Population

Vol. 161 Waste Issues

Vol. 162 Staying Fit

Vol. 164 The AIDS Crisis

Vol. 166 Marriage and Cohabitation

Vol. 168 Privacy and Surveillance

Vol. 172 Racial and Ethnic Discrimination

Vol. 173 Sexual Health

Vol. 174 Selling Sex

Vol. 175 Citizenship and Participation

Vol. 176 Health Issues for Young People

Vol. 177 Crime in the UK

Vol. 178 Reproductive Ethics

Vol. 179 Tackling Child Abuse

Vol. 180 Money and Finances

Vol. 181 The Housing Issue

Vol. 182 Teenage Conceptions

Vol. 183 Work and Employment

Vol. 184 Understanding Eating Disorders

Vol. 185 Student Matters

Vol. 186 Cannabis Use

Vol. 187 Health and the State

Vol. 188 Tobacco and Health

Vol. 189 The Homeless Population

Vol. 190 Coping with Depression

Vol. 191 The Changing Family

Vol. 192 Bereavement and Grief

Vol. 193 Endangered Species

Vol. 194 Responsible Drinking

Vol. 195 Alternative Medicine

Vol. 196 Censorship Issues

Vol. 197 Living with Disability

Vol. 198 Sport and Society

Vol. 199 Self-Harming and Suicide

Vol. 200 Sustainable Transport

Vol. 201 Mental Wellbeing

Vol. 202 Child Exploitation

Vol. 203 The Gambling Problem

Vol. 204 The Energy Crisis

Vol. 205 Nutrition and Diet

Vol. 206 Coping with Stress

Vol. 207 Consumerism and Ethics

Vol. 208 Genetic Modification

Vol. 209 Education and Society

Vol. 210 The Media

Vol. 211 Biotechnology and Cloning

Vol. 212 International Terrorism

Vol. 213 The Armed Forces

Vol. 214 Vegetarian Diets

Vol. 215 Religion in Society

Vol. 216 Tackling Climate Change

Vol. 217 Euthanasia and Assisted Suicide

Vol. 218 A Sustainable Future

Vol. 219 Class and Social Mobility

Vol. 220 Population Growth and Migration

Vol. 221 Equality and Gender Roles

Vol. 222 Tourism and Travel

Vol. 223 Crime. Punishment and Justice

Vol. 224 Domestic and Relationship Abuse

Vol. 225 LGBT Equality

Vol. 226 Globalisation and Trade

Vol. 227 Ethics in Business

Vol. 228 Illegal Drug Use

Vol. 229 Protecting Human Rights

Vol. 230 Evolution of the Internet

Vol. 231 The Abortion Debate

Vol. 232 Bullying in our Society

Vol. 233 Exploring Animal Rights

Vol. 234 Skin Deep - debating body image

Vol. 235 The Poverty Crisis

pain relief
and cannabis **186**.16
and the placebo effect **195**.28-9
see also palliative care
painkillers and sport **198**.28-9
paint, disposal of **161**.23
Pakistan, population growth **220**.2
Palermo Protocol (prevention of trafficking) **202**.2, 27;
229.17
palliative care **217**.10, 15-17, 18, 38
and assisted dying **217**.11, 17
availability **217**.15-16
effectiveness **217**.16
limitations **217**.10, 11, 16
Scotland **217**.18
palliative sedation **217**.3, 14, 25
palm oil industry and biodiversity **193**.8-9
pancreatitis **194**.6
panic attacks **206**.11, 16
paper **161**.5, 22
recycling **161**.24, 26
Paralympic Games **198**.20
talent identification **198**.22
parental child abduction **166**.36
parental leave **183**.18, 22, 24, 27; **191**.34, 39; **221**.4-5, 24
for adoption **178**.16
parental relationships
effect on children **166**.4-5, 29-32; **191**.1
and youth homelessness **189**.27
parental responsibility **166**.26-7, 34
cohabiting parents **166**.14-15
parental separation, effect on children **191**.1, 9
parenting orders **223**.32
parents
and adult children **191**.26-8
and alcohol
alcohol abuse **194**.27-8
influence on children's drinking **194**.25-6
attitudes to school learning styles **209**.1-3
and children's aggression **224**.22-3
and children's body image **234**.10
and children's education attainment **219**.26, 27, 33
and children's gambling **203**.13
and children's mental health **176**.29-30
cohabiting **166**.14-15
and corporal punishment **179**.30, 33, 35
death of a child **192**.20-23
empty nest syndrome disproved **191**.29
of lesbians and gays **225**.3-4
with mental health problems, effects on children
201.4, 8-9
parenting styles **191**.5
influence on children's character **191**.191.6
in prison, effects on children **201**.4
putting pressure on schools **209**.4
removing children from **179**.10-11
rights to information on sex offenders **179**.20-21
satisfaction with schools **209**.21
of sexually exploited children **202**.23
sex education role **182**.34-5
and smacking **179**.33

smoking, influence on young people smoking **188**.28
and stress
long working hours **206**.22-3
stay-at-home parents **191**.35
support for children's education **209**.36
support for first-time buyers **181**.1
supporting adult children **191**.26-8
and teenage depression **190**.27
young parents **182**.14-18
see also divorce; families; fathers; lone parents; mothers;
working parents
Paris, cycle hire **200**.31
Parkinson's disease and animal research **233**.36, 38
Parliament **175**.16-20
constituencies **175**.23-4, 26
elections **175**.22-9
need for reform to increase diversity **175**.21
public knowledge about **175**.16
women in **221**.13, 15, 20, 37
part-time jobs
and the gender pay gap **221**.24, 28
students **209**.32
partial (host) surrogacy **178**.7, 13
parties, political *see* political parties
passive euthanasia **217**.5
passive smoking **188**.5, 10-11, 12
passive victims of bullying **232**.8
pasteurization **211**.2
patents on GM seeds **208**.3-4
paternity leave **183**.18, 22, 24; **191**.34-5, 39; **221**.4-5
pathological gambling *see* problem gambling
patients
GP survey **187**.16-17
relationship with GPs **187**.31
rights **187**.13-15, 32-3
to refuse treatment **217**.13, 25
standards of care **187**.4, 26-8
patriotic hacking **196**.34-5
pay gap *see* gender pay gap
payday loans **235**.11
peace negotiations, female participation **221**.37
peer education programmes, HIV/AIDS **164**.18
peer mentoring, young parents **182**.39
peer pressure and drinking behaviour **194**.12
peer support and suicide **199**.33
penalties
cannabis supply **186**.2, 30
possession of cannabis **186**.1-2, 5, 9, 30
pensions
Army **213**.2
claiming after a death **192**.32-3
Europe **159**.25
saving for **159**.21, 22; **180**.8
UK **159**.3, 23, 25
universal social pension **159**.24
people smuggling **229**.18
permissive behaviour, effect of the media **196**.25-6
Perry pre-school programme **219**.35
personal information **168**.31
concerns about **168**.37
control of **168**.10-11, 31-2, 37; **230**.24, 30

and Data Protection Act **168**.10-11

protecting **168**.31-2, 37

personal privacy **168**.31-9

personalization of care **197**.13

pescetarian diet **214**.1

pest control and animal welfare **233**.4

pesticides

and GM crops **208**.3, 21, 23

and organic farming **205**.34, 35-6

petitions **175**.34-5

pets, exotic

demand for, impact on biodiversity in Asia **193**.20-21

impact on British wildlife **193**.39

pharmaceutical industry and GM crops **208**.21-2

pharmaceutical waste and water pollution **218**.38-9

phenazepam **228**.25

philanthropy **227**.20-21

Philippines, horse fighting **233**.27

philosophical beliefs, Equality Act definition **215**.24

phishing **230**.30

phobias **206**.11

in children **206**.13

treatment **206**.12-13

phone-hacking **210**.35-6

physical abuse

of children **179**.1-2, 5

as domestic abuse **224**.1, 3

of older people **159**.16

signs of **179**.5

of trafficked children **202**.29

physical disabilities **197**.3-5

physical punishment *see* corporal punishment

physician-assisted suicide (PAS)

doctors' opposition to **217**.22

prevalence **217**.24-5

see also assisted suicide

physiotherapists **197**.4

phytoplankton **193**.5

pica **184**.8

Pick's disease **201**.10

pig farming, mega-farms **233**.10-11

Pilates **162**.34

pill, contraceptive **176**.27; **182**.19

over the counter availability **182**.21-3

PIPA (Protect IP Act) **230**.35-6, 37

pipe smoking **188**.3

piracy on the Internet **230**.35-6

placebo effect **195**.28-9

and homeopathy **195**.26, 27, 29

planning laws and inequality **218**.3, 4

plastic bags **161**.5, 13-14, 19, 36-7

plastic surgery *see* cosmetic surgery

plastic waste **161**.5, 22, 29

recycling **161**.24, 29

Platform 51 **221**.28

play and disabled children **197**.37

playgrounds for older people **159**.39

pluripotent stem cells **211**.28, 35-7

see also embryonic stem cells; iPS cells

poisoning, emergency treatment **199**.14

poker, online **203**.28-9

police

drug classification, effects on policing **186**.36-7

and racism **172**.7-8

reporting a crime **223**.12

and Terrorism Act **212**.16

Policing and Crime Bill and prostitution **174**.1, 2

political debates, inclusion of the BNP **196**.7, 8

political material, Ofcom regulation **196**.19

political parties **175**.22

housing policies **181**.23

views on climate change **216**.25

politics

attitudes of girls and young women **175**.33-4

and middle classes **219**.10

older people's engagement in **159**.7

women's participation **221**.2, 13, 15, 20, 37

women's right to vote **221**.36

and young people **175**.30-32, 38-9

and the Internet **230**.9

see also elections; MPs; Parliament

poll card **175**.26

Vol. numbers appear first (in bold) followed by page numbers; a change in volume is preceded by a semi-**colon**.

Vol. 159	An Ageing Population	**Vol. 189**	The Homeless Population	**Vol. 212**	International Terrorism
Vol. 161	Waste Issues	**Vol. 190**	Coping with Depression	**Vol. 213**	The Armed Forces
Vol. 162	Staying Fit	**Vol. 191**	The Changing Family	**Vol. 214**	Vegetarian Diets
Vol. 164	The AIDS Crisis	**Vol. 192**	Bereavement and Grief	**Vol. 215**	Religion in Society
Vol. 166	Marriage and Cohabitation	**Vol. 193**	Endangered Species	**Vol. 216**	Tackling Climate Change
Vol. 168	Privacy and Surveillance	**Vol. 194**	Responsible Drinking	**Vol. 217**	Euthanasia and Assisted Suicide
Vol. 172	Racial and Ethnic Discrimination	**Vol. 195**	Alternative Medicine	**Vol. 218**	A Sustainable Future
Vol. 173	Sexual Health	**Vol. 196**	Censorship Issues	**Vol. 219**	Class and Social Mobility
Vol. 174	Selling Sex	**Vol. 197**	Living with Disability	**Vol. 220**	Population Growth and Migration
Vol. 175	Citizenship and Participation	**Vol. 198**	Sport and Society	**Vol. 221**	Equality and Gender Roles
Vol. 176	Health Issues for Young People	**Vol. 199**	Self-Harming and Suicide	**Vol. 222**	Tourism and Travel
Vol. 177	Crime in the UK	**Vol. 200**	Sustainable Transport	**Vol. 223**	Crime. Punishment and Justice
Vol. 178	Reproductive Ethics	**Vol. 201**	Mental Wellbeing	**Vol. 224**	Domestic and Relationship Abuse
Vol. 179	Tackling Child Abuse	**Vol. 202**	Child Exploitation	**Vol. 225**	LGBT Equality
Vol. 180	Money and Finances	**Vol. 203**	The Gambling Problem	**Vol. 226**	Globalisation and Trade
Vol. 181	The Housing Issue	**Vol. 204**	The Energy Crisis	**Vol. 227**	Ethics in Business
Vol. 182	Teenage Conceptions	**Vol. 205**	Nutrition and Diet	**Vol. 228**	Illegal Drug Use
Vol. 183	Work and Employment	**Vol. 206**	Coping with Stress	**Vol. 229**	Protecting Human Rights
Vol. 184	Understanding Eating Disorders	**Vol. 207**	Consumerism and Ethics	**Vol. 230**	Evolution of the Internet
Vol. 185	Student Matters	**Vol. 208**	Genetic Modification	**Vol. 231**	The Abortion Debate
Vol. 186	Cannabis Use	**Vol. 209**	Education and Society	**Vol. 232**	Bullying in our Society
Vol. 187	Health and the State	**Vol. 210**	The Media	**Vol. 233**	Exploring Animal Rights
Vol. 188	Tobacco and Health	**Vol. 211**	Biotechnology and Cloning	**Vol. 234**	Skin Deep - debating body image
				Vol. 235	The Poverty Crisis

pollinating insects, decliing numbers **193**.27-8

polling day **175**.24

pollution

effects on wildlife **193**.2

see also emissions; water pollution

polonium-210 in cigarette smoke **188**.9

polygamy and Islam **215**.12

pools **203**.4

Poor Laws **219**.11

poorism (slum tourism) **222**.16, 33-4

pop-culture tourism **222**.16

population

ageing population **159**.3, 6

global trends **159**.6

population changes

see ageing population; population growth

population growth **218**.26-30; **220**.1-15

controlling **218**.26-7; **220**.4, 10, 16-17, 19

developed countries **220**.1

developing countries **220**.2, 4

economic effects **220**.7

effects **220**.4, 5-7

and the environment **220**.4, 6-7, 14

and food supply **218**.29-30; 3-4, 6

growth rate **220**.1-2, 3, 13

projections **220**.2, 8-9

statistics **220**.4

and sustainability **218**.5

UK **220**.19

pornography **174**.19-26

effects **174**.19, 26

and the Internet **202**.18

children viewing **196**.38

women viewing **230**.2-3

and the law **174**.19-20, 21

statistics **174**.19

see also child pornography

porpoises, impact of climate change **193**.29

Portman Group **194**.39

Portugal, decriminalisation of drugs possession **228**.34

positive action

and age discrimination **159**.9-10

and racial discrimination **172**.17, 19

possession of drugs

cannabis **186**.1-2, 5, 9, 30; **228**.28-9

sentencing guidelines **228**.28-31

post-compulsory education

see A-levels; higher education; universities

post-mortem, hospital **192**.31

post-natal depression **190**.2, 14-17, 21-2

fathers **190**.16-17

mothers **190**.16-17

and suicide risk **190**.24

symptoms of **190**.14

post-traumatic stress disorder (PTSD) **176**.30; **201**.20-21

service personnel **213**.3-4, 5

therapies **213**.34

postal voting **175**.23

postgraduate destinations **185**.32

postgraduate study **185**.30

potatoes

genetically modified **208**.11

powering batteries **204**.39

poverty

and child labour **202**.4

and child trafficking **202**.27

children living in *see* child poverty

and children's wellbeing **191**.9

definitions **235**.1, 2-3

and disabled people **197**.35; **235**.5, 7

and education **209**.13-14, 34-5; **235**.21-2

pupil premium **209**.18

and free trade **226**.14, 29-30, 33

fuel poverty *see* fuel poverty

and girl's schooling **221**.39

global **226**.17; **235**.23-39

and global financial crisis **180**.1

and HIV/AIDS **164**.10, 27

lone parent families **191**.1

and mental health problems **201**.4

and Millennium Development Goals **218**.39; **235**.1-2, 25-7

and older people **159**.3; **235**.6, 8

and population growth **220**.6

reduction

through migration **226**.39

through trade **226**.28

rich-poor gap, UK **235**.12, 13

statistics **235**.5-8, 23, 24

and transport, developing countries **200**.13

in the UK **235**.1-22

and women **221**.34

see also child poverty; inequality

poverty cycle **235**.35

poverty tourism **222**.16, 33-4

power and control wheel **224**.7

power stations using biomass **204**.5, 7

Prader-Willi Syndrome **184**.8

pre-implantation genetic diagnosis **178**.2, 28-9, 30-31, 31-2

pre-marital sex, attitudes to **166**.1

pre-paid cards **180**.26

pregnancy **178**.2-3; **182**.3-5

and alcohol **194**.14

and dietary supplements **205**.4

and domestic abuse **224**.4-5

effects on unborn babies **224**.24, 37

employment rights **191**.37-8

and exercise **162**.32

and HIV **164**.3, 25, 27, 29-30, 31

myths **173**.5

pregnancy options counselling **231**.36-7

risks **182**.11, 37

and school **182**.6

and smoking **188**.11, 31

NHS anti-smoking strategies **188**.30-32

statistics **173**.3, 9

testing **182**.4-5

your choices **182**.6, 8-9

see also abortion; teenage pregnancies

prejudice

Islamaphobia *see* Islamophobia

against working classes **219**.3-4, 5-6
see also discrimination; homophobia
premature ejaculation **173**.2
premature babies, survival rate **231**.21, 22
presenteeism **183**.9
press
    press freedom, global study **196**.1-2
    press intrusion **168**.28-9
    press self-regulation, public support for **196**.6
    see also media
Press Complaints Commission **196**.3, 4-5
    Editor's Code **210**.27-8
    reform proposals **210**.29
    statement on phone-hacking **210**.36
press officers, political candidates **175**.26
Pretty, Diane **217**.1-2, 24
Prevent strategy (anti-terrorism) **212**.17-18
Prevention of Terrorism Act 2005 **212**.19
price of alcohol **194**.35
    minimum pricing **194**.36, 37
pricing
    Fairtrade prices **226**.36
    misleading practices **207**.15
Primary Care Trusts (PCTs) **187**.5
primates, endangered species **193**.22-3
Prime Minister **175**.17
prison
    and ex-service personnel **213**.4, 36, 37-9
    and the Human Rights Act **229**.5, 6
    and mental health, young people **201**.4
    prison leavers and homelessness **189**.6
    prison sentences **223**.19-20, 21
        not a deterrent for knife crime **223**.34
    prisoners' right to vote **229**.35-6
    suicide rate **199**.25
    women prisoners and self-harm **199**.12
    and work **223**.23
    and young people **223**.28-9
    see also youth custody
privacy **168**.1-3, 28-30
    definition **168**.1

Human Rights Act **196**.38
legal rights **168**.1, 2-3
and the media **210**.28, 33-9
    Human Rights Act **229**.5
and National Identity Scheme **168**.15
online **232**.28
protection, models of **168**.2
and social networking **168**.35-6; **210**.33-4; **230**.33-4
see also freedom of information
Privacy and Electronic Communications Regulations
    168.31
private healthcare **187**.24
private schools and children with learning problems
    197.15
pro-abortion (pro-choice) arguments **231**.1, 16
pro-eating disorder websites **184**.25-7
pro-life arguments **231**.1, 16
problem drinking *see* alcohol abuse
problem gambling **203**.2, 6, 19-39
    causes **203**.19
    children **203**.12, 15
    definition **203**.6, 12, 19
    genetic link **203**.30-31
    help **203**.21, 24-5, 34, 36
    Internet gambling **203**.28-9, 35-6
    people at risk **203**.23
    prevalence **203**.20
    signs **203**.2, 23
    social context **203**.32-3
    treatment **203**.24-5, 27
    women **203**.26, 35-6
    young people **203**.9-10, 11, 12, 15, 16
professions and social mobility **185**.38-9
prohibited steps order **166**.27, 35
promiscuity, international comparisons **173**.6
property crime **223**.4
property rights
    and cohabitation **166**.14
    disabled people **197**.21-2
proportional representation **175**.25
proscribed organizations **212**.15-16, 19

Vol. numbers appear first (in bold) followed by page numbers; a change in volume is preceded by a semi-**colon**.

Vol. 159 An Ageing Population
Vol. 161 Waste Issues
Vol. 162 Staying Fit
Vol. 164 The AIDS Crisis
Vol. 166 Marriage and Cohabitation
Vol. 168 Privacy and Surveillance
Vol. 172 Racial and Ethnic Discrimination
Vol. 173 Sexual Health
Vol. 174 Selling Sex
Vol. 175 Citizenship and Participation
Vol. 176 Health Issues for Young People
Vol. 177 Crime in the UK
Vol. 178 Reproductive Ethics
Vol. 179 Tackling Child Abuse
Vol. 180 Money and Finances
Vol. 181 The Housing Issue
Vol. 182 Teenage Conceptions
Vol. 183 Work and Employment
Vol. 184 Understanding Eating Disorders
Vol. 185 Student Matters
Vol. 186 Cannabis Use
Vol. 187 Health and the State
Vol. 188 Tobacco and Health

Vol. 189 The Homeless Population
Vol. 190 Coping with Depression
Vol. 191 The Changing Family
Vol. 192 Bereavement and Grief
Vol. 193 Endangered Species
Vol. 194 Responsible Drinking
Vol. 195 Alternative Medicine
Vol. 196 Censorship Issues
Vol. 197 Living with Disability
Vol. 198 Sport and Society
Vol. 199 Self-Harming and Suicide
Vol. 200 Sustainable Transport
Vol. 201 Mental Wellbeing
Vol. 202 Child Exploitation
Vol. 203 The Gambling Problem
Vol. 204 The Energy Crisis
Vol. 205 Nutrition and Diet
Vol. 206 Coping with Stress
Vol. 207 Consumerism and Ethics
Vol. 208 Genetic Modification
Vol. 209 Education and Society
Vol. 210 The Media
Vol. 211 Biotechnology and Cloning

Vol. 212 International Terrorism
Vol. 213 The Armed Forces
Vol. 214 Vegetarian Diets
Vol. 215 Religion in Society
Vol. 216 Tackling Climate Change
Vol. 217 Euthanasia and Assisted Suicide
Vol. 218 A Sustainable Future
Vol. 219 Class and Social Mobility
Vol. 220 Population Growth and Migration
Vol. 221 Equality and Gender Roles
Vol. 222 Tourism and Travel
Vol. 223 Crime, Punishment and Justice
Vol. 224 Domestic and Relationship Abuse
Vol. 225 LGBT Equality
Vol. 226 Globalisation and Trade
Vol. 227 Ethics in Business
Vol. 228 Illegal Drug Use
Vol. 229 Protecting Human Rights
Vol. 230 Evolution of the Internet
Vol. 231 The Abortion Debate
Vol. 232 Bullying in our Society
Vol. 233 Exploring Animal Rights
Vol. 234 Skin Deep - debating body image
Vol. 235 The Poverty Crisis

Islamic **212**.10
prostitution **174**.1-18
    arguments against **174**.5-7
    arguments for **174**.9-11
    children **174**.11-12; **202**.17, 24-6
    definition **174**.1
    government policies **174**.2
    and the law **174**.1-2, 3, 12-14
    public attitudes to **174**.4
    and rape **174**.5
    routes into **174**.3, 5, 10
    and sex trafficking **229**.19-20
    statistics **174**.2, 3
Protect IP Act (PIPA) **230**.35-6, 37
Protection for Harassment Act and workplace stress **206**.29
Protection of Animals Act 1911 **233**.1-2
Protection of Children Act, and film classification **196**.14
proteins **214**.34
    teenage requirements **176**.8
    and vegetarian diet **214**.12, 29, 30, 33
provocative victims of bullying **232**.8
Przewalski's horse **233**.26
psycho-social causes of homosexuality **225**.2
psychological abuse
    as domestic abuse **224**.3
    of older people **159**.16
psychological effects
    of cannabis **186**.7-8, 9-13, 16, 28-9, 30, 31, 32
    of human cloning **211**.27
    on trafficked children **202**.29
psychosis **201**.18-19
    and cannabis use **186**.10, 12, 13, 31, 32
psychotherapy
    and depression **190**.5, 11, 34
    and eating disorders **184**.37
    lack of availability **190**.37
psychotic depression **190**.2
pubic lice (crabs) **173**.17-18
public access to crime data **223**.1-2
public appointments, women **221**.14, 15
public attitudes
    to assisted suicide **217**.23, 34
    to biodiversity **216**.11; **218**.17
    to biotechnology **211**.5-6
    to burqa wearing **215**.39
    to business **227**.11, 13-14
    to citizenship ceremonies **175**.13-15
    to climate change **216**.21, 24, 25, 32
    to environmental issues **218**.14
    to film classification **196**.15-16
    to food from cloned animals **211**.6, 11, 12, 14
    to genetically modified food **208**.18, 29-30; **211**.5
    to human rights **229**.11-12
    to ID cards **168**.16
    to immigration **220**.22-3, 26, 27-8
    to inter-faith relations **212**.30-31
    to LGBT people **225**.11-13
    to marriage and cohabitation **166**.1-2
    to mental ill health **201**.23
    to Parliament **175**.16
    to population growth **220**.10
    to press self-regulation **196**.6
    to prostitution **174**.4
    to race and religion **172**.3
    on racial tension **172**.34
    to smacking **179**.32
    to social mobility and earnings **219**.15
    terrorism fears following London bombings **212**.4
    to use of torture **229**.12, 22
public figures and privacy **168**.36
public interest and media regulation **210**.28
public sector cuts **227**.16
public sector fraud **207**.21, 22
public services
    and National Identity Scheme **168**.16
    and population growth **220**.7
public transport
    and bicycles **200**.21
    city strategies **200**.30-31
    and disabled people **197**.11-12, 23
    effects of London bombings **212**.4
    high prices **200**.16
    passes and personal data monitoring **168**.9
    as terrorism targets **212**.7
    usage **200**.3
    see also buses; railways
puerperal psychosis **190**.15
pupil premium **209**.18, 24
pupils
    assaults on staff **209**.16
    attitudes to learning styles **209**.1-3
    attitudes to school **209**.11
    behaviour and teacher stress **209**.15

Q

qualifications
    academic and vocational **209**.1-3
    nurses **187**.33-5
    see also A-levels; degrees; educational achievement; GCSEs
Question Time (Parliament) **175**.19, 35
quitting smoking *see* smoking, giving up
Quorn **214**.9
    and vegan diet **214**.29

R

race
    definition **172**.1
    public attitudes to **172**.3
Race Online 2012 **230**.21
Race Relations Act **172**.4, 16
racial concentrations **172**.33
racial discrimination **172**.1-25
    definitions **172**.4-5, 8
    and drug laws **228**.34

against Gypsies and Travellers **172**.23
against Muslims **172**.35
what to do **172**.17
at work **172**.16-17
see also racism
racial diversity in schools **172**.36
racial equality
global public attitudes **229**.12
government strategies **172**.19, 20-21
racial harassment **172**.5, 17; **175**.7
racial tension
fuelled by media **172**.2, 10
public opinions **172**.34
racism **172**.1-2, 8
causes **172**.2
definition **172**.1, 8
effects **172**.1-2
at football matches **172**.2
forms of **172**.1
fuelled by media **172**.10
institutional **172**.6-8
against Jews **172**.24-5
and mental problems in young people **201**.2
against Muslims **172**.24
in the police **172**.7-8
racial harassment **172**.5, 17
on Twitter **232**.38
what to do **172**.2, 17
see also discrimination; employment and racism; ethnic
minorities; racial discrimination
racist bullying **172**.8; **232**.10, 11, 17
racist humour **172**.11-12
radiation exposure due to smoking **188**.9
radiative forcing (climate forcing) **216**.1
radicalism at universities **212**.13-14
radio
broadcasting regulations **210**.27
digital **210**.15
UK services **210**.3
RAF, and Strategic Defence and Security Review **213**.19
railways

and disabled people **197**.11
high-speed rail **200**.35, 36, 37-9
light rail **200**.30, 33-4
prices **200**.16
travel trends **161**.31-2
usage statistics **200**.3
rainforests *see* forests
rape
and prostitution **174**.5
statutory rape **173**.11
rapid-cycling bipolar disorder **201**.15
Rastafarianism and vegetarianism **214**.6
reality TV **210**.9
and body image **234**.7
reasonable adjustments for disabled people
education providers **197**.23
service providers **197**.21
workplace **197**.24
recession **180**.1-5
and abortion rate **231**.13
definition **180**.2
and employment **183**.1-2
and gender pay gap **221**.23
global **180**.1-2
impact on immigration **220**.31
indicators **180**.5
and lone parent families **191**.13
and students' plans **209**.31
reclassification of cannabis **186**.4-5, 32-3
public opinion **186**.31
recombinant DNA technologies *see* genetic modification
recovered memory of sexual abuse **179**.26-9
recovery programmes for offenders **223**.23-4
recruitment age, Armed Services **213**.15-16
recruitment of employees
Disability Symbol **197**.26-7
effects of recession **183**.1
use of social media **227**.38
recycling **161**.2, 18, 19, 22-9; **218**.11
employment in **161**.2
increase in **161**.31

negative effects **161**.35
organic waste *see* composting waste
organizations **161**.9
in public places **161**.20, 21
reducing emissions **161**.3
statistics **161**.22; **218**.12
targets **161**.20
red hair as cause of bullying **232**.16
red squirrels, Scotland **193**.37
Red Tractor assurance scheme **233**.3
REDD (Reducing Emissions from Deforestation in Devloping Countries) **218**.20-21
reduce, reuse, recycle **161**.7, 18; **218**.11
reducing waste **161**.18; **218**.11
incentives for **161**.38
redundancy
and disability discrimination **197**.24-5
emotional impact **183**.10-11
effect of recession **183**.2
refugees **235**.27
due to climate change **216**.10-11
see also asylum seekers
refuges **220**.36-7
environmental **220**.39
for male victims of domestic abuse **224**.11
for teenage victims of relationship abuse **224**.19
regeneration effect of tourism **222**.4
regenerative medicine
attitudes to **211**.6
see also embryonic stem cell research; stem cell research
regulation
animal experiments **233**.28, 33
of assisted suicide **217**.8
of broadcasters **196**.18-21
films **196**.13-16
of food additives **205**.15
of food labelling **205**.11-12
herbal medicine **195**.4, 33, 34-5, 37-8
Internet **196**.31, 36-7
media **210**.27-9, 34
obscene publications 22-3
press **196**.6
see also legislation
Rehabilitation of Offenders Act **223**.27
relational elements of marriage **166**.2-3
relationships
dissolution **166**.3
see also divorce
mixed-race **172**.30
effect of pornography **174**.26
problems **166**.7-8
and suicide **199**.24
and sex **173**.2
and sex education **173**.36, 37
and stress **206**.18
teaching about relationships **173**.36, 37
teenage, and violence **179**.19
trends **191**.3-4
see also marriage
relative poverty **235**.2-3
relaxation

and anxiety **206**.12
and stress **206**.34, 35
Release campaign for decriminalisation of drugs possession **228**.34
religion **215**.1-39
and abortion **231**.19, 39
attitudes to **212**.30-311 **215**.7-8
in Britain **215**.5-6, 8, 14, 15-16
and the Census **215**.5
and corporal punishment **179**.36
and discrimination **215**.23-5; **225**.34, 35
effects of **215**.7-8
and euthanasia **217**.2, 4, 6
faith schools *see* faith schools
funeral traditions **192**.34-6
and the law **215**.26-7
media coverage **215**.13
as natural human inclination **215**.16
religious observance in Britain **215**.5-6 ,8, 14, 15-16
statistics **215**.5-6
surveys **215**.5-6, 7-8, 15-16
in USA **215**.6
and vegetarianism **214**. 5, 6, 13
see also individual religions
religious discrimination at work **215**.23-4
religious education and faith schools **209**.23
religious freedom, global public attitudes **229**.12
religious marriage ceremonies **166**.6
religious offence **196**.11-12
religious organizations hosting civil partnerships **225**.32
religious prejudice, perception of **175**.7
religious slaughter **233**.16
religious tolerance **215**.23-39
and Islam **212**.32
religiously motivated crime
anti-Muslim hate crime **215**.28-30
remembrance of the deceased **192**.10
memorial websites **192**.38-9
see also funerals
remittances from migrants **220**.21, 35
remote gambling *see* online gambling
remote sensing **168**.26-7
remote working **227**.2-3
rendition of Libyan terror suspects **229**.22
renewable energy **204**.1, 2-8, 11-22, 25-7, 32; **218**.10
biofuels **204**.3, 26, 32, 34, 39
hydro power **204**.19, 27
microgeneration **204**.35-6
policies
EU **204**.30-31
UK **204**.7-8, 28-9
subsidies **204**.4
wave energy **204**.20, 26
see also energy efficiency; solar energy; wind energy
rented accommodation
as alternative to selling **181**.17
disability rights **197**.21-2
young people **181**.26, 33
reoffending rates
children **223**.31
and employment **223**.26

reparative therapy, homosexuality **225**.2

repayment mortgages **181**.28

repeat abortions **231**.11-12

reporters, female **210**.7

repossessed homes websites **181**.7

reproductive cloning **178**.36, 37; **211**.22, 24-7
   see also human reproductive cloning

research cloning **211**.32

residence of children after divorce **166**.35

resin, cannabis (hashish) **186**.2, 7, 9

resource consumption **218**.7-8, 13-14
   and population growth **220**.11-12, 14, 15
   water **218**.33

respiratory health
   and cannabis **186**.15, 28
   lung cancer **186**.15; **188**.6, 8
   and passive smoking **188**.5, 10-11
   and smoking **188**.5

responsible travel **222**.35
   definition **222**.25
   see also ecotourism

restorative justice **223**.28-9

retail industry
   and environmentalism **207**.34
   independent sector **207**.28
   packaging waste **161**.12
   plastic bags **161**.13-14
   statistics **207**.1

retargeting **230**.5

retirement
   feelings about **159**.15
   forced retirement **183**.14-15
   saving for **159**.21, 22; **180**.8
   spending patterns, retired people **159**.19
   working after retirement age **159**.10, 15
   see also pensions

reusing goods **161**.18; **218**.11

Reuters, social media guidelines **210**.32

Reverse Seasonal Affective Disorder **190**.7

rhinoceros, declining numbers **193**.1-2

rice, GM **208**.19, 29, 35

rich-poor gap
   global **226**.17-18
   UK **235**.12, 13

'right to buy' scheme, social housing **181**.25

right to die *see* assisted suicide; euthanasia

right to move, council tenants **181**.35-6

righteous eating fixation **184**.9

rights
   in abortion **231**.17, 18
   children's *see* children's rights
   consumer *see* consumer rights
   and the Internet **230**.30, 37, 38-9
   to privacy **168**.2-3; **196**.38
   sexual **196**.36, 38
   see also human rights

Rights of the Child, UN Convention on the **202**.2;
   229.24-6, 29

riots
   children's sentences **223**.29
   reasons for **223**.8
   young people's reactions **223**.9-11

RIRA (Real IRA) **212**.14

road accidents **200**.12
   see also drink-driving

road charging **200**.9, 10
   congestion charging **200**.17-18
   public attitudes **200**.6

road tax (Vehicle Excise Duty) **200**.7

road traffic
   pollution *see* pollution and transport
   see also cars

roads
   arguments against building new roads **200**.7-8
   economic effects of new roads **200**.8
   funding **200**.6, 7, 9-10
   patterns of use **200**.5
   shared by cars and bikes **200**.18
   see also road charging

Robin Hood tax **235**.13-15

roll-your-own cigarettes **188**.19

rough sleeping **189**.4, 16-17

Vol. numbers appear first (in bold) followed by page numbers; a change in volume is preceded by a semi-**colon.**

Vol. 159	An Ageing Population	Vol. 189	The Homeless Population	Vol. 212	International Terrorism
Vol. 161	Waste Issues	Vol. 190	Coping with Depression	Vol. 213	The Armed Forces
Vol. 162	Staying Fit	Vol. 191	The Changing Family	Vol. 214	Vegetarian Diets
Vol. 164	The AIDS Crisis	Vol. 192	Bereavement and Grief	Vol. 215	Religion in Society
Vol. 166	Marriage and Cohabitation	Vol. 193	Endangered Species	Vol. 216	Tackling Climate Change
Vol. 168	Privacy and Surveillance	Vol. 194	Responsible Drinking	Vol. 217	Euthanasia and Assisted Suicide
Vol. 172	Racial and Ethnic Discrimination	Vol. 195	Alternative Medicine	Vol. 218	A Sustainable Future
Vol. 173	Sexual Health	Vol. 196	Censorship Issues	Vol. 219	Class and Social Mobility
Vol. 174	Selling Sex	Vol. 197	Living with Disability	Vol. 220	Population Growth and Migration
Vol. 175	Citizenship and Participation	Vol. 198	Sport and Society	Vol. 221	Equality and Gender Roles
Vol. 176	Health Issues for Young People	Vol. 199	Self-Harming and Suicide	Vol. 222	Tourism and Travel
Vol. 177	Crime in the UK	Vol. 200	Sustainable Transport	Vol. 223	Crime. Punishment and Justice
Vol. 178	Reproductive Ethics	Vol. 201	Mental Wellbeing	Vol. 224	Domestic and Relationship Abuse
Vol. 179	Tackling Child Abuse	Vol. 202	Child Exploitation	Vol. 225	LGBT Equality
Vol. 180	Money and Finances	Vol. 203	The Gambling Problem	Vol. 226	Globalisation and Trade
Vol. 181	The Housing Issue	Vol. 204	The Energy Crisis	Vol. 227	Ethics in Business
Vol. 182	Teenage Conceptions	Vol. 205	Nutrition and Diet	Vol. 228	Illegal Drug Use
Vol. 183	Work and Employment	Vol. 206	Coping with Stress	Vol. 229	Protecting Human Rights
Vol. 184	Understanding Eating Disorders	Vol. 207	Consumerism and Ethics	Vol. 230	Evolution of the Internet
Vol. 185	Student Matters	Vol. 208	Genetic Modification	Vol. 231	The Abortion Debate
Vol. 186	Cannabis Use	Vol. 209	Education and Society	Vol. 232	Bullying in our Society
Vol. 187	Health and the State	Vol. 210	The Media	Vol. 233	Exploring Animal Rights
Vol. 188	Tobacco and Health	Vol. 211	Biotechnology and Cloning	Vol. 234	Skin Deep - debating body image
				Vol. 235	The Poverty Crisis

government targets **189**.8

and mental health **189**.11

young people **189**.23

see also homelessness

Royal Navy and Strategic Defence and Security Review **213**.18-19

Royal Mint **175**.2

Royal Standard **175**.2

RSPCA (Royal Society for the Prevention of Cruelty to Animals) **233**.1

rubbish *see* waste

runaways **189**.24, 25

running, effect on joints **162**.33

rural districts *see* countryside

S

SAD (Seasonal Affective Disorder) **190**.2, 6-7, 22

safe houses *see* refuges

Safe Routes to Schools (SRS) projects **200**.2

safe sex **173**.1, 5; **176**.22, 27, 28

see also contraception

safety

complementary and alternative medicine **195**.2, 12-13, 34, 37-8

and cycling **200**.21

and food additives **205**.15

food from cloned animals **211**.18, 19

of genetically modified food **208**.1, 2, 24

human cloning **211**.26, 27

and the Human Rights Act **229**.3

and self-harm **199**.6, 7-8

at work, young people **183**.28

safety and the Internet **232**.26-7; **230**.22-9

identity fraud **230**.24, 30

and National Identity Scheme **168**.15

social networking **179**.18; **230**.23-4

see also cyberbullying

Sainsbury's, plastic bags **161**.13

salaries

graduates **183**.36; **185**.32-4

young people's expectations **180**.21-2

see also earnings; wages

salmon, genetically modified **208**.31, 39

salt intake **205**.5

health effects **205**.25-6

need to reduce salt content of food **205**.18

Samaritans **176**.35; **199**.20, 22, 31, 35

same-sex relationships

adoption **225**.34

civil partnerships in religious buildings **225**.32

and domestic abuse **224**.5, 12-13

having a child **178**.9-10

human rights **229**.31-2

marriage **225**.33

sanitation in developing countries **218**.31-3, 36

Sarah's Law, dangers of **179**.20-21

SAT aptitude tests **219**.32

satellite surveillance **168**.26-7

Sativex **228**.26

saturated fats **205**.1, 3, 24

Saudi Arabia, death penalty **229**.37

savings

for old age **159**.21, 22; **180**.8

levels of **180**.7

savings accounts **180**.26

savings ratio **180**.7

saviour siblings **178**.28-31; **211**.32

scabies **173**.18-19

Schengen Information System **168**.9

schizo affective disorder **190**.9

schizophrenia **185**.8; **201**.16-17

and cannabis use **186**.10, 12, 31, 32; **228**.8

school bullying **232**.1, 5-6, 17

dealing with bullying **232**.4, 18

racist bullying **232**.10, 11, 17

staff experiencing cyberbullying **232**.33, 34-6

school leaving age and teenage pregnancies **182**.31

school meals provision, World Food Programme **229**.28

School Standard and Framework Act 1998 **225**.7

schools **209**.1-26

academies **209**.25, 26

admission systems **219**.24

assaults on staff **209**.16

attendance during pregnancy **182**.6

biometric fingerprinting **168**.30

and body image **234**.11, 21, 29-30

bullying *see* school bullying

carbon footprint reduction **200**.19-20

and CCTV **168**.25

and cervical cancer vaccination **173**.38-9

and children in poverty **235**.22

children's attitudes to **209**.1-3, 11

citizenship teaching **175**.32, 37

curriculum reform **209**.5

developing countries **229**.27-8

and disabled children **197**.5, 23

children with learning problems **197**.14-15

and ending violence against women and girls **224**.29

employers' involvement **219**.26

ex-service personnel as mentors **213**.32

faith-based **209**.22-3, 24; **215**.17-22

and financial education **180**.38-9

free schools **209**.19-21

faith-based **215**.21-2

girl's non-attendance **221**.38-9

and healthy eating **205**.6-7

ICT education **230**.13

journeys to **200**.1-2, 19-20

knife crime education **223**.16-17

and LGBT people **225**.5-8

parent satisfaction **209**.21

parental presuure **209**.4

and physical activity **162**.13

and racial diversity **172**.36-7

school system reform **209**.6

school type and pupil's degree perfomance **219**.32

selective, and social mobility **219**.31

self-harm support **199**.5-6

sex education *see* sex education

and sexual health services **173**.29, 30; **182**.31

single-sex **221**.30-32

and social mobility **219**.18, 23, 28, 31

and special educational needs **197**.14-15, 23

sports, Olympic-style competition **198**.5

standards **209**.7-10

and stress **176**.37, 38-9

support for children with suicidal feelings **199**.31, 33

travel plans **200**.2

and violent extremism **212**.12

vocational courses **183**.31

weighing children **162**.16

see also education; National Curriculum; secondary schools; teachers

Scotland

abortion law **231**.3

crime statistics **223**.2

drug assessment for NHS use **187**.23

drug strategy **228**.24

euthanasia legislation rejection **217**. 30

feelings of Scottish identity **175**.13

census question **175**.10-11

gangs and knife crime **223**.6-7

health service **187**.30

homelessness **189**.3

homophobic crime **225**.30

life on the streets **189**.18-20

palliative care **217**.18

red squirrels **193**.37

reintroduction of animals **193**.33-4

Scottish parliament, submitting a petition **175**.35

suicides **199**.26

teenage abortions **182**.2

teenage pregnancy **182**.2, 7

sea level rise **216**.9, 16-17, 20-21

effect on island nations **220**.38

seal hunting **233**.22-3

seas *see* marine environments

Seasonal Affective Disorder (SAD) **190**.2, 6-7, 22

SeaWorld, slavery case **233**.21

second generation children, cultural identity **172**.29

second-hand smoke *see* passive smoking

secondary schools

see A-levels; GCSEs; schools

secondment **183**.18

secret self and self-harm **199**.11

secularism

as argument for banning burqa **215**.36

in Britain **215**.15

security

as reason for banning burqa **215**.35

and social networking **210**.30-31

select committees **175**.18-19

selective schools and social mobility **219**.31

selenium

in red meat **214**.34-5

and vegetarian diets **214**.29

self-affirmation **199**.6; **234**.3

self-blame *see* blame, feelings of

self build projects **181**.30-31

self-defence and protection against bullying **232**.21

self-directed violence *see* self-harm; suicide

self-employment, graduates **185**.30

self-esteem

Dove campaign **234**.33

see also body image

self-harm **176**.30, 33-5; **190**.28-9; **199**.1-19

avoidance techniques **199**.5-6, 7, 8

and bullying **232**.9

case studies **199**.9

and depression **190**.23

definition **199**.1, 4, 20

effects **199**.11

minimizing damage **199**.7

prevalence **199**.4

reasons **199**.2, 5, 10-12

risk factors **199**.4

risk groups **199**.1-2, 4-5

sources of help **199**.2-3, 5

self-help **199**.2, 5-6, 7, 8

and suicide **199**.12, 23-4

Vol. numbers appear first (in bold) followed by page numbers; a change in volume is preceded by a semi-colon.

Vol. 159 An Ageing Population

Vol. 161 Waste Issues

Vol. 162 Staying Fit

Vol. 164 The AIDS Crisis

Vol. 166 Marriage and Cohabitation

Vol. 168 Privacy and Surveillance

Vol. 172 Racial and Ethnic Discrimination

Vol. 173 Sexual Health

Vol. 174 Selling Sex

Vol. 175 Citizenship and Participation

Vol. 176 Health Issues for Young People

Vol. 177 Crime in the UK

Vol. 178 Reproductive Ethics

Vol. 179 Tackling Child Abuse

Vol. 180 Money and Finances

Vol. 181 The Housing Issue

Vol. 182 Teenage Conceptions

Vol. 183 Work and Employment

Vol. 184 Understanding Eating Disorders

Vol. 185 Student Matters

Vol. 186 Cannabis Use

Vol. 187 Health and the State

Vol. 188 Tobacco and Health

Vol. 189 The Homeless Population

Vol. 190 Coping with Depression

Vol. 191 The Changing Family

Vol. 192 Bereavement and Grief

Vol. 193 Endangered Species

Vol. 194 Responsible Drinking

Vol. 195 Alternative Medicine

Vol. 196 Censorship Issues

Vol. 197 Living with Disability

Vol. 198 Sport and Society

Vol. 199 Self-Harming and Suicide

Vol. 200 Sustainable Transport

Vol. 201 Mental Wellbeing

Vol. 202 Child Exploitation

Vol. 203 The Gambling Problem

Vol. 204 The Energy Crisis

Vol. 205 Nutrition and Diet

Vol. 206 Coping with Stress

Vol. 207 Consumerism and Ethics

Vol. 208 Genetic Modification

Vol. 209 Education and Society

Vol. 210 The Media

Vol. 211 Biotechnology and Cloning

Vol. 212 International Terrorism

Vol. 213 The Armed Forces

Vol. 214 Vegetarian Diets

Vol. 215 Religion in Society

Vol. 216 Tackling Climate Change

Vol. 217 Euthanasia and Assisted Suicide

Vol. 218 A Sustainable Future

Vol. 219 Class and Social Mobility

Vol. 220 Population Growth and Migration

Vol. 221 Equality and Gender Roles

Vol. 222 Tourism and Travel

Vol. 223 Crime. Punishment and Justice

Vol. 224 Domestic and Relationship Abuse

Vol. 225 LGBT Equality

Vol. 226 Globalisation and Trade

Vol. 227 Ethics in Business

Vol. 228 Illegal Drug Use

Vol. 229 Protecting Human Rights

Vol. 230 Evolution of the Internet

Vol. 231 The Abortion Debate

Vol. 232 Bullying in our Society

Vol. 233 Exploring Animal Rights

Vol. 234 Skin Deep - debating body image

Vol. 235 The Poverty Crisis

treatment **199**.13-14, 15
  young people **176**.33-5
self help
  anxiety problems **206**.12
  housing **181**.32
  for stress **206**.3-4, 27
self-image *see* body image
self-loathing as cause of self-harm **199**.10
self management training and bipolar disorder **190**.11
self-poisoning, emergency treatment **199**.14
self-regulation of the press **196**.6
self-stigma, mental illness **201**.28
semen and fertility problems **178**.4-5
sensory impairment and age **159**.4
sentencing **223**.19-20, 21
  children **223**.29, 30
  community sentences **223**.20, 23
  for drugs offences **228**.23, 28-31
  Legal Aid, Sentencing and Punishment of OffendersA
  Bill **223**.25
  and maturity of young offenders **223**.33-4
  terrorism offences **212**.9-10, 19
separation
  effect on children **166**.4-5, 29-31, 32; **191**.1, 9
  see also divorce
serotonin and mental health **201**.33
sex and cannabis use **186**.29
sex discrimination
  in the Army **213**.13-14
  see also gender inequality
sex education **173**.7, 31-7; **182**.28-9, 32-5
  and LBGT relationships **225**.7
  role of parents **182**.34-5
sex object culture **174**.27-8
  and lads' magazines **174**.29-30
sex offences, statistics **223**.5
sex offenders
  disclosure of **179**.20-21
  help for **179**.22-3
  registration, and Human Rights Act **229**.6
sex-selection abortion **231**.18, 30-31
sex tourism **202**.18-19
sex trafficking **229**.17
  and prostitution **229**.19-20
sexting **221**.9-10; **230**.26-7
sexual abuse **173**.11; **179**.2-3, 13-29
  and children's mental health problems **201**.3
  as domestic abuse **224**.1, 3
  effects **179**.24-5
  false memories **179**.26-9
  getting help **179**.25
  and the Internet **179**.15-17
  of older people **159**.16-17
  signs of **179**.5
  statistics **179**.13, 15, 17
sexual abusers *see* paedophiles; sex offenders
sexual behaviour **173**.3, 6
  and alcohol **194**.19, 23
  teenagers **173**.8-10, 12-14; **182**.1
  worries about sex **173**.1, 2
sexual bullying **221**.11

sexual content on the Internet **196**.36-9
  child abuse **196**.39
sexual exploitation of children **202**.16-31
  case study **202**.24-6
  effects of **202**.22-3
  perpetrators **202**.20-21
  and sex tourism **202**.18-19
  see also child pornography; child prostitution
sexual health **173**.23-39; **176**.21-8
  being ready for sex **173**.2; **176**.21-2
  and cannabis use **186**.29
  safe sex **173**.1, 5; **176**.22, 27, 28
  sexual dysfunction **176**.23
  see also contraception; sexually transmitted infections
sexual health services in schools **173**.29, 30; **182**.31
sexual offences, statistics **223**.5
Sexual Offences Act **174**.1
sexual orientation **225**.1-18
  altering **225**.2, 16, 17-18
  attitudes to **225**.11-13
  and bullying *see* homophobic bullying
  causes **225**.1-2, 15-16
  definitions **225**.3, 5, 19-20
  discovering **225**.1
  discrimination **225**.9-10, 28-9, 35
  and eating disorders in men **184**.13
  and the law **225**.28-39
  and US military **225**.38-9
  see also gay men; lesbians; LGBT people; transgender
  people
Sexual Orientation Change Efforts (SOCE) **225**.17-18
sexual rights **196**.36
  threats to **196**.38
sexualisation
  effect of the media **196**.25-6
  and lads' magazines **174**.29-30
  of women **174**.27-8; **221**.34
  of young girls **174**.38-9; **221**.9-10
sexuality *see* sexual orientation
sexually transmitted infections (STIs) **173**.17-23; **176**.23,
  24-8
  attitudes to **173**.22
  avoiding **176**.24, 26
  bacterial vaginosis **173**.17
  chlamydia **173**.17, 20; **176**.25, 26
  effects on fertility **178**.5
  genital warts **173**.18, 20-21
  gonorrhoea **173**.18, 21
  hepatits **173**.18
  herpes **173**.18, 21
  HIV/AIDS **173**.21
  knowledge about **173**.10, 25
  molluscum contagiosum (water warts) **173**.18
  prevention **173**.23, 24
  pubic lice (crabs) **173**.17-18
  scabies **173**.18-19
  statistics **173**.3, 9-10, 15-16, 20-21
  symptoms **173**.17-19
  syphilis **173**.19, 21
  testing for **173**.26-8
  thrush **173**.19

---

men **188**.1, 3
    effects of smoking 15
  passive smoking **188**.5, 10-11, 12
  and pregnancy **182**.15; **188**.11, 30-32
  prevalence **188**.1-3
  pro-smoking views **188**.34-5
  and stress **206**.33
  students **185**.9
  women **188**.1, 3
    effects of smoking **188**.15
    pregnant women **182**.15; **188**.11, 30-32
  young people **176**.4, 12-13
    influences on smoking habits **188**.24-8
    prevention **176**.13
    stopping smoking **188**.13-14
smoothies, and fluid intake **205**.28
smuggling, tobacco **188**.23
snuff **188**.11
social care services
  and older people **159**.4, 28, 26, 29
social capital and health **219**.12
social class
  and health **219**.11-13
  middle classes **219**.1-2, 9-10
  working classes **219**.3-4, 5-6
  and alcohol consumption, teenagers **194**.24
  and children's nutrition **162**.13-14
  and educational attainment **219**.29-30
  and obesity **162**.5
  see also social mobility
social drinking **194**.17
social exclusion **235**.2
  older people **159**.30
  and sexual orientation **225**.9-10
social factors
  and gambling **203**.32-3
  and suicide **199**.24
social gambling **203**.12
social housing
  attitudes to **181**.14
  and children **181**.9-11
  demand for **181**.29
  effects of **181**.9-11; 33-5
  and immigrants **181**.12; **220**.28, 29
  quality **181**.10
  shortage **181**.8
social isolation
  older people **159**.3, 8, 17, 30
social marketing
  and reducing consumption **161**.34
  and sex education **182**.39
social mobility **219**.14-39
  and education **219**.18, 22, 23, 25-6, 27-8, 34-5
  government strategy **219**.17-21
  and higher education **185**.18
  perceptions of **219**.15
  prejudice against **219**.4
  and the professions **185**.38-9
  rate of **219**.14
Social Mobility and Child Poverty Commission **219**.19
social model of disability **197**.2

social networking **210**.5, 12, 14
  and bullying **232**.25, 26-7, 28
  and business ethics **227**.37-9
  and gambling **203**.17
  and gender **230**.2, 3
  and privacy **168**.34-6; **210**.33-4; **230**.33-4
  and relationship abuse **224**.16-17
  reporting inappropriate content **232**.35
  Reuters guidelines **210**.32
  safety **179**.18; **230**.23-4
  security issues **210**.30-31
  and travel **222**.9
social security benefits *see* state benefits
social status and ageing **159**.32
social welfare
  history **219**.11
  see also state benefits
social welfare law problems and mental health, young people **201**.29-30
socio-economic groups
  and academic performance **209**.13-14
  and higher education participation **209**.34-5
  and life expectancy **188**.18
  and obesity **162**.5
  and smoking **188**.2, 3, 33
  see also social class
sociosexuality index **173**.6
sofa surfing **189**.7
soft drinks **205**.5, 28
Soil Association **205**.33
solar energy
  solar electricity **204**.3, 25, 35–6
  from space **204**.39
  subsidies **204**.7
  water heating **204**.3, 21-2, 25, 35
soldiers, child *see* child soldiers
solicitors
  and divorce **166**.35
  and mediation **166**.39
solvent and volatile substance abuse **228**.7, 15
somatic-cell nuclear transfer (SCNT) **211**.24
  see also therapeutic cloning
SOPA (Stop Online Piracy Act) **230**.35-6, 37
South Africa as gap year destination **222**.19
sovereign debt **226**.5
spa holidays 5
space, solar energy collection **204**.39
space tourism **222**.17-18
SPCA (Society for the Prevention to Cruelty to Animals) **233**.1
Speaker of the House of Commons **175**.17-18
Special Educational Needs (SEN) **197**.14-15, 23
species conservation, zoos **233**.25, 26
species loss **193**.13; **220**.6
  England **193**.31-2
  Galapagos Islands **193**.24-5
spending **180**.7
  and budgeting **180**.30-31
  on communications **210**.12
  on holidays **222**.5, 6-7
  household **207**.7, 8

older people **159**.19

personal **207**.6

sperm cell creation

from stem cells **178**.39

sperm donation **178**.10-12

concerns about **178**.12

donor contact with offspring **178**.25-7

effects of removing donor anonymity **178**.24

spiking drinks **194**.8-10

spin doctors **175**.26

spina bifida **197**.3

sponsorship and advertising to children **207**.39

sport **198**.1-39

betting **203**.8

and bullying **232**.1-2, 7

and drugs *see* drugs in sport

and inclusion **198**.18-26

sports events and sex trafficking **229**.20

trends **198**.1-17

see also Olympic Games

Sport England, funding for disability sport **198**.18

spot-reduction of fat **162**.33

spread betting **203**.4

squatting **181**.20

squirrels

grey **193**.38

red, Scotland **193**.37

SSRIs (Selective Serotonin Re-Uptake Inhibitors)
190.10, 32-3

stakeholder theory of corporate social responsibility
227.10

stalking **224**.5

stamp duty **181**.24

political party policies **181**.23

stamps, UK **175**.2

standing orders **180**.14

starchy foods **205**.2-3

start-ups, business **227**.5

state benefits

benefit fraud **219**.5-6

after bereavement **192**.30-31, 32

disabled people **197**.31-4

benefit cuts **229**.32

maternity pay **191**.38

and National Identity Scheme **168**.16, 18

and welfare reform bill **235**.9

see also disability benefits

state pension **159**.3, 23

statements of special education needs **197**.23

statutory homelessness **189**.3-4

Statutory Maternity Pay **191**.38

statutory rape **173**.11

staycations **222**.5

steel cans recycling **161**.27

stem cell lines **211**.30

stem cell research **178**.38; **211**.29-37

embryonic **178**.33-7; **211**.29-32

ethical issues **178**.33-5; **211**.30-31, 34

humanist view **178**.36-7

induced pluripotent stem cells **178**.38; **211**.35-7

stem cell therapy **211**.30

for multiple sclerosis **211**.38-9

stem cell transplants, saviour siblings **178**.28-31; **211**.32

stem cells **211**.28, 29-30

embryonic **211**.28, 29-30, 35-6

from aborted fetuses **211**.33

iPS **211**.35-7

tissue-specific (adult) **211**.28, 29

stepfamilies **191**.10

sterilization **182**.19

and fertility **178**.4

steroids *see* anabolic agents/steroids

stimulants (uppers) **228**.3

signs of use **228**.14

and sports drug abuse **198**.29

see also ecstasy

stomach cancer, effect of salt intake **205**.26

stop and search

anti-Muslim discrimination **212**.28-9

racial differences **172**.7

Terrorism Act **212**.16

stopping cannabis use **186**.11

stopping smoking *see* smoking, giving up
store cards **180**.14, 26
    and personal data **168**.8
straddling bus **200**.29
street design for sustainable transport **200**.30
street homelessness **189**.18-20
    young people **189**.27-8
Street View (Google) and privacy **210**.33
stress
    causes **206**.17-31
    complications **206**.4
    coping with **206**.32-9
    definition **206**.24
    and exams **176**.5, 38-9
    and exercise **162**.37
    and fertility **178**.5
    school stress **176**.37, 38-9
    self help **206**.3-4, 27
    signs and symptoms **206**.1-2, 7-9, 17, 19
    statistics on **206**.5, 21
    stay-at-home parents **191**.35
    students **206**.38-9
    treatment **206**.2-4
    work-related *see* work-related stress
strokes **159**.4
    effect of salt intake **205**.25
    stem cell therapy **211**.33
students
    accommodation **181**.18, 19-20; **185**.7; **209**.30
    dropping out **209**.32
    health issues **176**.5-6
    housing **185**.7
    lifestyle **209**.30-33
    mental health **185**.8
    and money matters **180**.28-9, 32-3; **209**.31-2
        budgeting **180**.30-31; **185**.3, 11
        costs of a university education **185**.11, 17, 36
        financial help **206**.39
        graduate starting salaries **185**.33-4
        grants **180**.28, 33; **185**.2
        income and expenditure **180**.32-3
        loans **180**.28, 33; **185**.2
    satisfaction with course **185**.4-5
    and stress **206**.38-9
    student life **185**.3-4
study leave **183**.18
submissive victims of bullying **232**.8
subsidies
    definition **226**.30
    impact on developing countries **226**.33
substance abuse
    and depression **190**.3
    and homelessness **189**.10-11
    and prostitution **174**.3
    and sex **173**.15
    see also alcohol; drug abuse; solvent abuse
sugar
    in diet **205**.3
    labelling rules **205**.12
suicidal feelings **199**.23
    and bullying **232**.9

children **176**.35, 36-7
getting help **199**.20, 22, 28
how to help someone **199**.22, 25-6, 30, 32-3
reasons **199**.20, 24, 30
young people **190**.29
suicide **199**.20-39
    and anti-depressants **190**.24
    and bullying **232**.9
    copycat suicides **199**.36
    and depression **190**.21, 23
    and the Internet **199**.33, 35
    and the media **199**.35, 36
    myths **199**.27
    reasons for **199**.24, 30
    risk factors for **199**.20-21, 31-2
    risk groups **199**.20-21, 24-5
    and self-harm **199**.12, 23-4
    statistics **190**.27; **199**.21
    suicide terrorism
        condemned by Islam **215**.10-11
        Great Britain **212**.5-6
        use of children **212**.11-12
    support for suicidal people **199**.20, 22, 26, 30
        children **199**.33
        men **199**.38
        Samaritans **199**.20, 22, 31, 35
    warning signs **190**.26-7; **199**.22, 25, 29-30, 31-2
    young people **190**.26, 27; **199**.21, 31-3
    see also assisted suicide; physician-assisted suicide (PAS)
Suicide Act and assisted suicide **217**.24
sunbeds and cancer **176**.10-11
superbugs, hospital **187**.28-9
super-farms **233**.3, 9-11
supermarkets
    and banana prices **226**.35
    and meat free products **214**.7
    packaging waste **161**.12
    and plastic bags **161**.13-14
    threat to local shops **207**.26, 27
    vegetarian food availability **214**.9
support groups
    gamblers **203**.25,
    sexual abusers **179**.22-3
    stress and anxiety sufferers **206**.3, 12
surgery, weight loss **162**.3
surgical abortion **231**.7
surrogacy **178**.7-8, 13-14
    and same-sex couples **178**.10
    success rate **178**.14
surveillance
    by the government **168**.4-5, 7-8, 13-14, 27, 35
    and law **168**.10-11
    by local authorities **168**.20-21
    online **168**.32-3
    risks **168**.4
    by satellite **168**.26-7
suspended prison sentences **223**.19
sustainability
    cities **218**.6
    fisheries **218**.23

and marine environments **218**.22
and population growth **218**.5
and resource use **218**.7-8
sustainable agriculture **214**.14, 20-21
sustainable development **226**.3-4
sustainable housing **181**.39
sustainable tourism **222**.8-9, 21-3
definition **222**.25
sustainable transport networks **200**.30-31
swearing on television **196**.21
synthetic biology, public attitudes **211**.5
syphilis **173**.19, 21

T

talent identification
Olympic sports **198**.8-10
Paralympic sports **198**.22
talking
about dying **192**.8, 24
and the grieving process **192**.5
see also communication
talking therapies **190**.5, 11, 34
tapenadol, classification **228**.25
tar, in cigarette smoke **188**.4
effect on heart **188**.7
effect on lungs **188**.5
tariffs **226**.13, 26-7
taxation **180**.24
air travel **222**.14-15
after death **192**.32
ending 50p rate **219**.7
as ethical investment issue **227**.33
on financial sector **235**.13-15
high earners opinions of **227**.25
landfill tax **161**.12, 20, 35
and multination corporations **227**.32-3
and road building **200**.7
on savings interest **180**.26
tax havens **227**.34-6

tobacco **188**.23
and trade **226**.13, 26-7
taxis and disabled people **197**.12
tea, and fluid intake **205**.27
teachers
assaults by pupils **209**.16
attitudes to school learning styles **209**.1-3
concerns about CCTV in schools **168**.25
and cyberbullying **232**.33, 34-6
faith schools **209**.23
influence on children's attainment **219**.33
not encouraging Oxbridge applications **185**.24
stress caused by pupil behaviour **209**.15
technology use
business trends **227**.1-3
Middle Britain **219**.2
teenage depression **190**.25-7, 30
teenage magazines and sexualisation **174**.39
teenage mothers **182**.16
supervised homes **182**.17-18
teenage parents **182**.14-18
see also teenage fathers; teenage mothers
teenage pregnancies **173**.3, 9; **176**.4; **182**.1-13
and abortion **182**.12-13
options **182**.6, 8-9
public perceptions of **182**.13
risks **182**.11, 37
statistics **182**.2, 7, 10-11, 37
Teenage Pregnancy Strategy **182**.24, 25-6, 27
teenage relationship abuse **224**.4, 16-21, 35-6
teenage suicide, warning signs **190**.26-7
teenagers *see* young people
teeth and human diet **214**.12
teetotallers **194**.11-12
telecommunications
broadband services **210**.15; **230**.6-8
international comparisons **210**.13-15
prices, international comparisons **210**.14-15
statistics **210**.10
trends **210**.4-5, 10-16
telephones

Vol. numbers appear first (in bold) followed by page numbers; a change in volume is preceded by a semi-**colon**.

Vol. 159 An Ageing Population
Vol. 161 Waste Issues
Vol. 162 Staying Fit
Vol. 164 The AIDS Crisis
Vol. 166 Marriage and Cohabitation
Vol. 168 Privacy and Surveillance
Vol. 172 Racial and Ethnic Discrimination
Vol. 173 Sexual Health
Vol. 174 Selling Sex
Vol. 175 Citizenship and Participation
Vol. 176 Health Issues for Young People
Vol. 177 Crime in the UK
Vol. 178 Reproductive Ethics
Vol. 179 Tackling Child Abuse
Vol. 180 Money and Finances
Vol. 181 The Housing Issue
Vol. 182 Teenage Conceptions
Vol. 183 Work and Employment
Vol. 184 Understanding Eating Disorders
Vol. 185 Student Matters
Vol. 186 Cannabis Use
Vol. 187 Health and the State
Vol. 188 Tobacco and Health

Vol. 189 The Homeless Population
Vol. 190 Coping with Depression
Vol. 191 The Changing Family
Vol. 192 Bereavement and Grief
Vol. 193 Endangered Species
Vol. 194 Responsible Drinking
Vol. 195 Alternative Medicine
Vol. 196 Censorship Issues
Vol. 197 Living with Disability
Vol. 198 Sport and Society
Vol. 199 Self-Harming and Suicide
Vol. 200 Sustainable Transport
Vol. 201 Mental Wellbeing
Vol. 202 Child Exploitation
Vol. 203 The Gambling Problem
Vol. 204 The Energy Crisis
Vol. 205 Nutrition and Diet
Vol. 206 Coping with Stress
Vol. 207 Consumerism and Ethics
Vol. 208 Genetic Modification
Vol. 209 Education and Society
Vol. 210 The Media
Vol. 211 Biotechnology and Cloning

Vol. 212 International Terrorism
Vol. 213 The Armed Forces
Vol. 214 Vegetarian Diets
Vol. 215 Religion in Society
Vol. 216 Tackling Climate Change
Vol. 217 Euthanasia and Assisted Suicide
Vol. 218 A Sustainable Future
Vol. 219 Class and Social Mobility
Vol. 220 Population Growth and Migration
Vol. 221 Equality and Gender Roles
Vol. 222 Tourism and Travel
Vol. 223 Crime. Punishment and Justice
Vol. 224 Domestic and Relationship Abuse
Vol. 225 LGBT Equality
Vol. 226 Globalisation and Trade
Vol. 227 Ethics in Business
Vol. 228 Illegal Drug Use
Vol. 229 Protecting Human Rights
Vol. 230 Evolution of the Internet
Vol. 231 The Abortion Debate
Vol. 232 Bullying in our Society
Vol. 233 Exploring Animal Rights
Vol. 234 Skin Deep - debating body image
Vol. 235 The Poverty Crisis

communications database **168**.13-14
   mobile *see* mobile phones
television
   and body image **234**.7, 19
   offensive language **196**.21, 24
   reality television *see* reality television
   regulation **196**.18-20; **210**.27
   UK services **210**.3
   viewing habits **210**.4, 11
telomeres and ageing **159**.32, 33; **162**.12
temperature of the earth
   changes **216**.8, 9
   measurement **216**.26-7
   see also climate change; global warming
temporary accommodation **189**.8
temporary class drug orders **228**.25
tenancy sustainment services **189**.34
tenants
   council tenants' rights to move **181**.35-6
   rights **181**.16
terminally ill people
   assisted suicide *see* assisted suicide
   and carer's grief **192**.6
   euthanasia *see* euthanasia
termination *see* abortion
Territorial Army (TA) **213**.30
territorial privacy **168**.2
terrorism **212**.1-39
   counter-terrorism **212**.15-25
      legislation **212**.15-16, 19, 20
      police powers **212**.15-16
      review **212**.21-2, 26, 38-9
   definition **212**.1, 15
   effects **212**.2-3
   and identity cards **168**.16, 18
   and Islam **212**.32
   Islamist **212**.8-10
   London bombings **212**.4, 5
   reasons for **212**.1
   and satellite surveillance **168**.27
   suicide terrorism
      Great Britain **212**.5-6
      use of children **212**.11-12
   Terrorism Acts **212**.15-16, 19
   Terrorism Prevention and Investigation Measures Bill **212**.20
   in the UK **212**.5-7, 8-10
      effect on the public **212**.4
      by Irish Republican groups **212**.14
      by Islamists **212**.8-10
test tube babies *see* in vitro fertilisation
testicles and fertility problems **178**.5
tetrahydrocannabinol *see* THC
Tetra Pak cartons, recycling **161**.23
text message bullying **232**.17, 29
textiles recycling **161**.25, 28
THC (delta-9 tetrahydrocannabinol)
   and cannabis strength **186**.7, 22
   effects **186**.9
   in skunk **186**.13
therapeutic cloning **178**.34; **211**.9, 22-3

humanist view of **178**.36-7
   research applications **211**.23
therapeutic use exemption, drugs in sport **198**.28
thermohaline circulation **216**.8
Third World *see* developing countries
threats as domestic abuse **224**.1
thrush **173**.19
tidal power **204**.26
tigers
   as endangered species **193**.1, 18
   tiger tourism **222**.26
timber production, environmental impact **193**.4
timber recycling **161**.25
time limit for abortion **231**.21-3
time management, and stress **206**.18, 34, 35
tins, recycling **161**.27
tissue specific (adult) stem cells **211**.28, 29
tobacco
   advertising ban **188**.23
   chemical contents of smoke **188**.4, 9-10, 15
   and the economy **188**.22-3
   see also smoking
tobacco industry **188**.23
   tobacco pickers' health problems **188**.39
tobacco-specific nitrosamines (TSNAs) **188**.11
toll roads **200**.9, 10
tools, recycling **161**.25
top jobs, gender gap **221**.13-22
torture
   public attitudes to **229**.12, 22
   UK complicity in **229**.21-3
   by US soldiers **212**.36-7
tourism
   alternative **222**.16, 24
   Britain as holiday destination **222**.2-3, 5, 11
   child sex tourism **202**.18-19
   and climate change **216**.12
   destination choice **222**.2-3, 11
   economic benefits **222**.4-5, 28, 30
   and endangered species **222**.26
   environmental impact **222**.21, 22, 25, 27, 28, 29
   and ethics **222**.31-2
   gap year destinations **222**.19
   holiday spending **222**.5, 6-7
   and London Olympics **222**.12-13
   slum tourism **222**.16, 33-4
   space tourism **222**.17-18
   sustainable tourism **222**.8-9, 21-3, 25
   trends **222**.1-3, 8-9
   volunteer tourism **222**.8, 27-8, 36-9
   see also ecotourism; holidays; responsible tourism
toxic chemicals in tobacco smoke **188**.4, 9-10, 15
toxicity
   and GM crops **208**.27
   nanotechnology **208**.16
toys, colour coding and gender **221**.7-8
trade
   definition **226**.26
   international *see* international trade
trade in endangered species **193**.20-21
   ivory trade ban **193**.19

trade footprint **226**.34

trade justice **226**.29, 33

trade liberalisation *see* free trade

traditional medicine **195**.9, 10

    regulation difficulties **195**.36

traffic pollution *see* pollution and transport

trafficking **174**.14-18; **229**.17-20

    children **202**.27-31

    definition **202**.1

    EU laws **179**.29

    and prostitution legalisation **174**.6, 14, 15

    support for victims of sex trafficking **174**.16-17

    in UK **202**.27-9, 30, 31

training

    and age discrimination **159**.9

    effect of recession **183**.2

    young people **183**.29

trams **200**.29, 33, 34

tranquilizers **194**.9

    and phobia treatment **206**.13

Transatlantic Trends survey **220**.22-3

transgender people **225**.5, 19-27

    definitions **225**.19-20

    and domestic abuse **224**.5, 12-13

    experiences **225**.21-2

    hate crime against **225**.30-31

    and marriage **225**.27

transgenic technology *see* genetic modification

Transition to Adulthood (T2A) Alliance **223**.33

transnational corporations (TNCs) **226**.1, 27

transphobia **225**.7-8

transport **200**.1-39

    and disabled people **197**.11-12, 23

    electric vehicles **200**.26-9

    emissions *see* emissions

    and the environment **200**.14-39

    of food, environmental impact **205**.31

    and global poverty **200**.13

    and inequality **218**.3, 4

    noise **200**.14-15, 22

    policies **200**.15

    and schools **200**.1-2, 19-20

    sustainable transport networks **200**.30-31

    trends **161**.31-2; **200**.1-13

    see also air travel; cars; public transport; railways

transsexual people

    definition **225**.19

    and marriage **225**.27

    public figures **225**.25-6

transvestites **225**.19

trauma as cause of anxiety **206**.11

travel agents **222**.3

travel behaviour **222**.3

travel health advice **222**.10

travel information sources, new technologies **222**.9

travellers' cheques **180**.13-14

treatment

    anxiety problems **206**.12

    bipolar disorder **190**.10-11; **201**.15

    depression **190**.26, 31-9

    drug abuse effects **228**.2

    drug dependency **228**.16-18

    eating disorders **184**.6-7, 29-39

    of homosexuality **225**.2, 16, 17-18

    obesity **162**.2-3, 6, 20

        see also weight management

    panic attacks **206**.16

    phobias **206**.12-13

    psychosis **201**.18-19

    Seasonal Affective Disorder **190**.6-7

    stress **206**.2-4

    see also self help

tricyclic antidepressants **190**.10-11, 33

Trojan gene effect **208**.39

trolling **232**.32, 37

tuberculosis and HIV **164**.30

tuition fees, university **185**.11, 17, 29, 36

12 Step Programme **184**.30; **203**.25

twins, IVF, and health problems **178**.21-2

Twitter **210**.18

    and racist abuse **232**.38

two signature rule, abortions **231**.2

Vol. numbers appear first (in bold) followed by page numbers; a change in volume is preceded by a semi-**colon**.

Vol. 159 An Ageing Population	**Vol. 189** The Homeless Population	**Vol. 212** International Terrorism
Vol. 161 Waste Issues	**Vol. 190** Coping with Depression	**Vol. 213** The Armed Forces
Vol. 162 Staying Fit	**Vol. 191** The Changing Family	**Vol. 214** Vegetarian Diets
Vol. 164 The AIDS Crisis	**Vol. 192** Bereavement and Grief	**Vol. 215** Religion in Society
Vol. 166 Marriage and Cohabitation	**Vol. 193** Endangered Species	**Vol. 216** Tackling Climate Change
Vol. 168 Privacy and Surveillance	**Vol. 194** Responsible Drinking	**Vol. 217** Euthanasia and Assisted Suicide
Vol. 172 Racial and Ethnic Discrimination	**Vol. 195** Alternative Medicine	**Vol. 218** A Sustainable Future
Vol. 173 Sexual Health	**Vol. 196** Censorship Issues	**Vol. 219** Class and Social Mobility
Vol. 174 Selling Sex	**Vol. 197** Living with Disability	**Vol. 220** Population Growth and Migration
Vol. 175 Citizenship and Participation	**Vol. 198** Sport and Society	**Vol. 221** Equality and Gender Roles
Vol. 176 Health Issues for Young People	**Vol. 199** Self-Harming and Suicide	**Vol. 222** Tourism and Travel
Vol. 177 Crime in the UK	**Vol. 200** Sustainable Transport	**Vol. 223** Crime, Punishment and Justice
Vol. 178 Reproductive Ethics	**Vol. 201** Mental Wellbeing	**Vol. 224** Domestic and Relationship Abuse
Vol. 179 Tackling Child Abuse	**Vol. 202** Child Exploitation	**Vol. 225** LGBT Equality
Vol. 180 Money and Finances	**Vol. 203** The Gambling Problem	**Vol. 226** Globalisation and Trade
Vol. 181 The Housing Issue	**Vol. 204** The Energy Crisis	**Vol. 227** Ethics in Business
Vol. 182 Teenage Conceptions	**Vol. 205** Nutrition and Diet	**Vol. 228** Illegal Drug Use
Vol. 183 Work and Employment	**Vol. 206** Coping with Stress	**Vol. 229** Protecting Human Rights
Vol. 184 Understanding Eating Disorders	**Vol. 207** Consumerism and Ethics	**Vol. 230** Evolution of the Internet
Vol. 185 Student Matters	**Vol. 208** Genetic Modification	**Vol. 231** The Abortion Debate
Vol. 186 Cannabis Use	**Vol. 209** Education and Society	**Vol. 232** Bullying in our Society
Vol. 187 Health and the State	**Vol. 210** The Media	**Vol. 233** Exploring Animal Rights
Vol. 188 Tobacco and Health	**Vol. 211** Biotechnology and Cloning	**Vol. 234** Skin Deep - debating body image
		Vol. 235 The Poverty Crisis

U

UDAW (Universal Declaration on Animal Welfare) **233**.2

UK
  child exploitation **202**.1-2
  and children's rights **229**.24, 29-30
  climate change impacts **216**.9
  climate change targets **216**.33
  counter-terrorism strategy **212**.17-18
    review **212**.21-2, 38-9
  economy **227**.3
  endangered species **193**.31-9
  energy policy **204**.7-8, 28-9
  genetically modified crops **208**.5, 17-18, 25-6
  immigration **220**.20-21, 24-5
  NHS provision differences **187**.29-30
  population goals **220**.19
  poverty **235**.1-22
  terrorism **212**.4, 5-7, 8-10, 14
  and torture complicity **229**.21-3
  tourism **222**.1-3, 4-5, 11
  trade initiatives **226**.28
  trafficked children **202**.27-9, 30, 31
  see also entries under British

umbilical cord
  blood storage **178**.33
  stem cells **178**.28

underage drinking **176**.17-18
  see also young people and alcohol

underage gambling **203**.12-14

undergraduates *see* students

underground travel and disabled people **197**.12

underoccupation and housing benefit cuts **235**.9

unemployment **235**.6
  and adult children living with parents **181**.4
  as reason for return migration **220**.34
  and social housing **181**.35
  statistics **227**.16
  young people **183**.37-8

UNESCO, education programmes **229**.28

UNICEF
  End Child Exploitation campaign **202**.2
  projects **229**.24-6

Unilever, advertising **234**.22-3

Union Flag **175**.2

unipolar (endogenous) depression **190**.10, 22-3

UNISON **187**.21

United Nations (UN)
  body image event **234**.37
  business and human rights **227**.27, 28
  climate change conferences **216**.37, 38, 39
  Committee on the Rights of the Child, and corporal punishment **179**.30, 31
  Convention on the Rights of the Child **202**.2; **229**.24-6, 29
  Economic and Social Commission for Western Asia (ESCWA) **229**.28
  education programmes **229**.28
  encouraging vegan diet **214**.24
  Environment Programme (UNEP) **193**.10-11, 13
  and human rights of lesbian, gay, bisexual and transgender people **229**.31-2
  Palermo Protocol (prevention of trafficking) **229**.17
  Population Fund (UNFPA) **229**.28
  public attitudes to UN role in human rights **229**.11
  REDD rainforest protection programme **218**.20-21
  Strategic Drugs Policy Review **186**.38

units of alcohol **176**.15; **194**.4-5, 14
  recommended safe limits **194**.8, 14, 18

Universal Declaration of Human Rights **229**.1
  and business **227**.28
  and privacy **168**.3

universal social pension **159**.24

universities **209**.27-39
  application numbers **209**.37-8
    from state schools **185**.19-20
  business involvement **185**.34-6
  comparing standards **185**.26-8
  and extremism **212**.13-14
  funding **209**.29, 31-2, 35
  government policy framework **185**.25
  predictor of degree results **219**.32
  school background of students **185**.19-20
  and social class **209**.34-5
  and social mobility **185**.18-20
  student finance **180**.28-9, 32-3; **209**.31-2
  student life **209**.30-33
  university structure reform **185**.20-21

urban areas
  and sustainability **218**.6
  sustainable transport networks **200**.30-31

urine testing in sport **198**.27

USA
  armed forces and sexual orientation **225**.38-9
  Charter Schools **209**.20
  criticism of NHS **187**.19-20
  death penalty **223**.39; **229**.37
  environmental impact **193**.5
  and euthanasia **217**.2, 11
  online piracy laws **230**.35-6
  privacy rights **168**.3
  religious belief **215**.6

V

vaccines
  benefits of **233**.33
  production from GM plants **208**.21-2
  search for AIDS vaccine **164**.34-6

vascular dementia **201**.10

veganism **214**.1, 2, 3
  and children **214**.28
  and health **214**.37
  and heart-related diseases **214**.33
  reasons for **214**.3; **233**.2
  United Nations encouragement of **214**.24

vegetables *see* fruit and vegetables

vegetarian diets **214**.1, 2

vegetarianism **205**.37-8; **214**.1-39

and children **214**.28, 36
definition **214**.1, 28
and the environment **214**.15-27
and health **214**.5, 12, 28-9, 31-2, 38-9
history of **214**.4
and religion **214**.5, 6, 13
reasons for becoming vegetarian **214**.4-5, 13
types of vegetarianism **214**.1, 2
verbal abuse, shouting at children **179**.39
vertical occupational segregation **221**.27
victimisation **172**.5, 17; **225**.28
definition **221**.3
of mental health sufferers **201**.22
victims of bullying **232**.2, 8
characteristics **232**.2, 8, 31
effects of bullying **232**.3, 8, 21, 25, 26
feelings **232**.21, 26
what to do **232**.18, 26
victims of crime
mental health sufferers **201**.22
and restorative justice **223**.29
role in justice system **223**.24
victims of domestic abuse **224**.2
disabled people **224**.4
getting help **224**.38
LGBT people **224**.5, 12-13
male **224**.5, 9-10, 11
older people **224**.4
pregnant women **224**.4-5
reasons for not leaving **224**.6
young people **224**.4, 16-21, 24, 25
women **224**.2, 3-4, 11
video games, age ratings **196**.17
Video Recordings Act 1984 **196**.14
videos
cyberbullying **232**.29
and data protection **232**.35
see also films
violence
against girls **221**.37, 38
against Muslims **215**.28-30

against school staff **209**.16
by children **224**.22-3
at football grounds **198**.13
and gangs **223**.6-7, 13-15
and life on the streets **189**.27-8
and mental ill health **201**.22, 26
as obscenity **196**.22
and prostitution **174**.3, 5
against women **221**.37
and young people **176**.4
see also corporal punishment; domestic abuse; physical
abuse
violent crime, trends **223**.4
violent extremism
condemned by Islam **215**.10
in schools **212**.12
in universities **212**.13-14
vitamins
B vitamins **214**.34
in meat **214**.34
supplements **205**.4; **214**.10, 29
and teenage diet **176**.8-9
and vegetarian diet **205**.38; **214**.28, 29, 30, 33
vitamin D **214**.34
vocational qualifications
attitudes to **209**.1-3
at schools **183**.31
see also specialist diplomas
vocational training
and age discrimination **159**.9
and gender **221**.28
voice, children's rights to **229**.25-6
volatile substance abuse *see* solvent abuse
voluntary activity
graduates **185**.31
volunteer tourism **222**.8, 27-8, 36-9
young people **175**.32, 39
voting
compulsory **175**.28-9
eligibility to vote **175**.23
lowering voting age **175**.36-7, 39

making it easier **175**.26-7
   Parliamentary elections **175**.22-9
   prisoners' right to vote **229**.35-6
   women's right to vote **221**.36
vulnerable employment, developing countries **235**.26
vulnerable people and assisted dying legalization **217**.7-8,
   12, 19, 32, 33, 39

W

wages
   footballers **198**.12
   garment industry **229**.13
   high earners' attitudes to **227**.24-5
   inequality **227**.15, 16
   minimum wage, young people **183**.28
   public perceptions of wage levels **219**.15
   soldiers **213**.1
   see also earnings; incomes; salaries
WAGs (footballers wives and girlfriends) **198**.15-17
waist measurement and exercise **162**.36
Waitrose, plastic bags **161**.14
Wales
   abortion law **231**.3
   drug strategy **228**.24
   health service **187**.30
   homelessness **189**.4
   teenage pregnancy **182**.2, 7, 10-11
walking
   to school **200**.7
   see also exercise
Wallace, Bethaney **234**.36
Wan, Gok **234**.19
war
   as cause of migration **220**.36-7
   and public grief **192**.7-8
Warsi, Baroness Sayeeda **215**.31-2
waste **218**.11-12
   amounts **161**.1, 3-5, 22
   collection **161**.6
   definition **161**.1
   electronic **218**.15-16
   and energy generation **161**.20, 38, 39; **204**.6, 24
   food **161**.4, 10-11, 19; **205**.31, 32
   government strategy **161**.20
   hazardous **161**.1, 6, 32; **218**.12
   household **218**.11-12
   incineration **161**.7
   reducing waste **161**.18, 19, 20, 38; **218**.11
   sorting **161**.25
   see also household waste; landfill; litter; organic waste;
     recycling
waste hierarchy **161**.7, 18; **218**.11
water consumption **205**.27-8
   and the environment **205**.32
   labelling of bottled waters **205**.11
   reducing **218**.34-5
   statistics **218**.36-7
water filters, recycling **161**.25
water pollution **218**.38-9

water power **204**.19, 27
water supplies
   and agriculture **214**.17
   and climate change **216**.6, 10
   drinking water access, developing countries **218**.31-3, 36
   freshwater resources **193**.5
   and GM crops **208**.20
   and population growth **220**.6
   scarcity **218**.33
water warts **173**.18
wave energy **204**.20, 26
wealth
   inherited **219**.8
   and teenage drinking **194**.24
weapons
   gun crime **223**.5
   knife crime *see* knife crime
weather
   events of 2010 **216**.5, 13
   predictions, UK **216**.9
websites
   blocking **196**.38
   and child sexual abuse **179**.17
   newspapers **210**.19
   promoting eating disorders **184**.25-7
   and self-harm **199**.19
   selling repossessed properties **181**.7
weight loss
   dieting **205**.22-3
   drug treatment **162**.2-3, 6, 20
   and exercise **162**.20, 36
   financial incentives **162**.22-3
   and lifestyle changes **162**.20
   and Quorn **214**.9
   as sign of eating disorder **184**.30
   surgery **162**.3
weight management **176**.7
welfare reform bill **235**.9, 10
welfare support *see* state benefits
Western countries *see* developed countries
whales
   animal rights **233**.20, 21
   hunting **193**.1
   impact of climate change **193**.29
   whale watching holidays **222**.26
wheelchairs **197**.11
   wheelchair sport **198**.20-21
white British pupils, poverty and academic performance
   209.13-14; **219**.29-30
white people as targets of racism **172**.2
WikiLeaks **210**.20-26
wild animals
   in circuses **233**.4, 14-15
   reintroduction in Britain **193**.33-4
wildlife
   butterflies, Britain **193**.36
   impact of chemicals **193**.16-17
   impact of non-native species **193**.12, 38-9
   London **193**.35
   and organic farming **205**.35
   reintroduction of species, Britain **193**.33

species loss, England **193**.31-2
tourism **222**.26
trade **193**.20-21
see also conservation; endangered species; extinction
wills **192**.24, 25-7
living *see* advance directives
wind farms **204**.13-18
costs **204**.17-18
impacts on local communities **204**.12
offshore **204**.14-18
under-performance **204**.13, 18
wind power **204**.3, 11-18, 25-6; **218**.10
EU targets **204**.11
microgeneration **204**.35
UK targets **204**.8, 17
winter deaths, older people **159**.4
winter fuel payments **204**.23
withdrawal symptoms, gambling **203**.6
withdrawing medical treatment **217**.14
womb damage and fertility **178**.4
women
and abortion **231**.18-19
right to choose **231**.17, 25
and ageing population **159**.5
and alcohol **194**.7, 14
increasing consumption **176**.14
pregnant women **194**.14
and Armed Forces **213**.12-14
aspiring to be WAGS **198**.15-17
body image concerns **234**.14-15
career aspirations **221**.21
credit card usage, global **180**.19
dieting, effect on daughters **184**.21-2
as domestic abuse perpetrators **224**.9-10
as domestic abuse victims **224**.2, 3-4, 11
eating disorders in over 40s **184**.14-15
and fertility *see* fertility
financial implications of partner's death **192**.33
and financial independence **180**.17-18
and gambling
online gambling **203**.35-6

as target of gaming companies **203**.26
gender pay gap **221**.22-5, 27-8, 35-6, 37
glass ceiling **221**.21-2
and HIV/AIDS **164**.5-6
in pregnancy **164**.3, 25, 27, 29-30, 31
and household finance roles **180**.18-19
and household tasks **221**.6
and inequality **221**.1-2, 33-6, 37
Internet usage **230**.2-3
marriage expectations **166**.3
marriage risks **166**.11
maternity leave **183**.18, 21, 23, 24
media usage **210**.12
migrant workers **174**.17-18; **220**.35
Muslim
and face veils **215**.34-9
as victims of hate crime **215**.29
and the news **210**.6-8
older women and IVF **178**.17, 19-20
and politics **221**.2, 13, 15, 20, 36, 37
post-natal depression **190**.2, 14-15, 21-2
pregnant women
dietary supplements **205**.4
and smoking **188**.11, 30-32
and provocative clothing **221**.12
rights, global public attitudes **229**.12
and sex object culture **174**.27-8, 30
and sexually transmitted infections (STIs) **173**.23
shopaholism **207**.6
and smoking **188**.1, 3, 15
in pregnancy **188**.11, 30-32
and stress **206**.8-9
voting rights **221**.36
see also girls and young women; mothers; pregnancy;
working mothers
women in the workforce
boardroom positions **221**.14, 15, 16, 17-18, 21-2, 37
effect of children on career **183**.21
equal pay *see* gender pay gap
glass ceiling **221**.21-2
mothers preferring not to work **183**.25

Vol. numbers appear first (in bold) followed by page numbers; a change in volume is preceded by a semi-**colon**.

Vol. 159   An Ageing Population
Vol. 161   Waste Issues
Vol. 162   Staying Fit
Vol. 164   The AIDS Crisis
Vol. 166   Marriage and Cohabitation
Vol. 168   Privacy and Surveillance
Vol. 172   Racial and Ethnic Discrimination
Vol. 173   Sexual Health
Vol. 174   Selling Sex
Vol. 175   Citizenship and Participation
Vol. 176   Health Issues for Young People
Vol. 177   Crime in the UK
Vol. 178   Reproductive Ethics
Vol. 179   Tackling Child Abuse
Vol. 180   Money and Finances
Vol. 181   The Housing Issue
Vol. 182   Teenage Conceptions
Vol. 183   Work and Employment
Vol. 184   Understanding Eating Disorders
Vol. 185   Student Matters
Vol. 186   Cannabis Use
Vol. 187   Health and the State
Vol. 188   Tobacco and Health

Vol. 189   The Homeless Population
Vol. 190   Coping with Depression
Vol. 191   The Changing Family
Vol. 192   Bereavement and Grief
Vol. 193   Endangered Species
Vol. 194   Responsible Drinking
Vol. 195   Alternative Medicine
Vol. 196   Censorship Issues
Vol. 197   Living with Disability
Vol. 198   Sport and Society
Vol. 199   Self-Harming and Suicide
Vol. 200   Sustainable Transport
Vol. 201   Mental Wellbeing
Vol. 202   Child Exploitation
Vol. 203   The Gambling Problem
Vol. 204   The Energy Crisis
Vol. 205   Nutrition and Diet
Vol. 206   Coping with Stress
Vol. 207   Consumerism and Ethics
Vol. 208   Genetic Modification
Vol. 209   Education and Society
Vol. 210   The Media
Vol. 211   Biotechnology and Cloning

Vol. 212   International Terrorism
Vol. 213   The Armed Forces
Vol. 214   Vegetarian Diets
Vol. 215   Religion in Society
Vol. 216   Tackling Climate Change
Vol. 217   Euthanasia and Assisted Suicide
Vol. 218   A Sustainable Future
Vol. 219   Class and Social Mobility
Vol. 220   Population Growth and Migration
Vol. 221   Equality and Gender Roles
Vol. 222   Tourism and Travel
Vol. 223   Crime. Punishment and Justice
Vol. 224   Domestic and Relationship Abuse
Vol. 225   LGBT Equality
Vol. 226   Globalisation and Trade
Vol. 227   Ethics in Business
Vol. 228   Illegal Drug Use
Vol. 229   Protecting Human Rights
Vol. 230   Evolution of the Internet
Vol. 231   The Abortion Debate
Vol. 232   Bullying in our Society
Vol. 233   Exploring Animal Rights
Vol. 234   Skin Deep - debating body image
Vol. 235   The Poverty Crisis

in senior positions **183**.12; **221**.13-22
see also working mothers
Women Chainmakers of Cradley Heath **221**.35
wood, recycling **161**.25
wood fuelled heating **204**.36
woodland planting on landfill sites **161**.33
work
 effects of cannabis use **186**.10
 effect on fathers' involvement with children **191**.33
 and homelessness **189**.33
  Big Issue selling **189**.37-9
 in prison **223**.23
 past retirement age **159**.10, 15
 workers' rights **229**.14-16
 see also child labour; employment; migrant workers
work and gender *see* gender and work
work-family balance, fathers **191**.34-5
work-life balance **183**.16-17, 22-3
 see also hours of work
Work Positive **206**.26
work-related stress **183**.6-7; **206**.7-9, 17-18, 24-9
 causes **206**.29
 costs **183**.6-7; **206**.5
 legislation **206**.25, 28-9
 signs **206**.7-9
work-to-live cycle **180**.23
workforce monitoring by GPS **168**.27
working age dementia **201**.10-11
Working Better project **183**.27
working class
 discrimination against **172**.25
 prejudice against **219**.3-6
working conditions, developing countries
 garment industry, campaign for living wage **229**.13
 improvement initiatives **226**.28
working hours *see* hours of work
working mothers **191**.36
 effects on children **221**.26
 maternity rights **191**.37-8
 preferring not to work **183**.25
 and social housing **181**.10
working parents **191**.30-39
 and stress **206**.22-3
workplace
 absences **183**.8, 9
 age discrimination **159**.8-13
 and disabled people **197**.20-21, 24-5, 26-7
 drug misuse signs **228**.15
 exercise **162**.23, 24
 gender balance **221**.19
  boardroom positions **221**.14, 15, 16, 17-18, 20, 21-2, 37
 obesity discrimination **162**.21
 monitoring **168**.9, 38
 new technology and working practices **227**.1-3
 racial discrimination **172**.16-17, 18
 sexual orientation discrimination **225**.9, 28-9
 stress *see* work-related stress
workplace bullying **232**.23, 24
 cyberbullying **227**.38
World Anti-Doping Agency (WADA) **198**.31, 32

World Bank **226**.9-10
 and gender equality **221**.2
 and poverty reduction **235**.23-4, 32
world food supply, and GM crops **208**.19, 23-4, 32, 34-6
World Health Organization
 criticism of homeopathy **195**.30-31
 mental health programmes **201**.8-9
World Trade Organization (WTO) **226**.1, 7-8, 14-15
 criticism of **226**.14-15, 32
 trade rules **226**.27

Y

YMCA, homelessness projects **189**.22
young carers **201**.8-9
young children
 body image **184**.27
 sexualisation of girls **174**.38-9; **221**.9-10
young offenders
 maturity as a factor in sentencing **223**.33-4
 and prison **223**.28-9
young onset dementia **201**.10-11
young parents **182**.14-18
 housing rights **189**.25
young people
 and age discrimination **159**.12
 in the Armed Forces **213**.15-16
 attitudes to diversity **172**.37
 attitudes to Europe **175**.12
 attitudes to higher education **209**.27-8
 attitudes to HIV **164**.18
 attitudes to marriage **166**.1-2
 attitudes to riots **223**.9, 10-11
 and body image **184**.17-18; **234**.7, 26
 and British identity **175**.12
 and the Budget **180**.24
 and cannabis
  anti-drug helpline criticised **186**.26-7
  effect on families **186**.23-5
  mental health effects **186**.10, 29
  penalties for possession **186**.1-2, 5, 9, 30
  worldwide use **186**.19
 and citizenship **175**.30-39
 and cosmetic surgery **234**.33, 34
 and crime *see* young offenders; youth crime
 and criminal justice system **223**.25
  maturity as a factor in sentencing **223**.33-4
 and cyberbullying **232**.30-32
 and depression **190**.25-30
 and disability **197**.16-17, 36-7
 and domestic abuse **179**.19; **224**.16-26
  teenage relationship abuse **224**.4, 16-21, 35-6
 and drug abuse **176**.18; **228**.1
  treatment **228**.17
 eating disorders **184**.21-2, 30-31
 and employment **180**.20
 entrepreneurial aspirations **227**.6
 financial problems **180**.34-6
 and gambling **203**.9-18
  Internet gambling **203**.16-18

Vol. numbers appear first (in bold) followed by page numbers; a change in volume is preceded by a semi-**colon.**